Glitter Artistry

Glitter Artistry
Bags, Tags & Cards

Barbara Trombley

A LARK / CHAPELLE BOOK
A Division of Sterling Publishing Co., Inc.
New York / London

A Lark/Chapelle Book

Chapelle, Ltd., Inc.
P.O. Box 9255, Ogden, UT 84409
(801) 621-2777 • (801) 621-2788 Fax
e-mail: chapelle@chapelleltd.com
Web site: www.chapelleltd.com

Created and produced by Red Lips 4 Courage Communications, Inc.
www.redlips4courage.com
Eileen Cannon Paulin
President
Catherine Risling
Director of Editorial

10 9 8 7 6 5 4 3 2

Published by Lark Books, A Division of
Sterling Publishing Co., Inc.
387 Park Avenue South, New York, N.Y. 10016

First Paperback Edition 2008
©2006 by Barbara Trombley

Distributed in Canada by Sterling Publishing,
c/o Canadian Manda Group, 165 Dufferin Street
Toronto, Ontario, Canada M6K 3H6

Distributed in the United Kingdom by GMC Distribution Services,
Castle Place, 166 High Street, Lewes, East Sussex, England BN7 1XU

Distributed in Australia by Capricorn Link (Australia) Pty Ltd.,
P.O. Box 704, Windsor, NSW 2756 Australia

ISBN 13: 978-1-60059-000-9 (hardcover) 978-1-60059-215-7 (paperback)
ISBN 10:1-60059-000-4 (hardcover) 1-60059-215-5 (paperback)

For information about custom editions, special sales, premium and
corporate purchases, please contact Sterling Special Sales Department
at 800-805-5489 or specialsales@sterlingpub.com.

Foreword

Have you ever seen your name in glitter? My first experience with glitter was when I was 7 years old. My mother gave me a Christmas ornament with my name on it in large, glittering letters. I'd gaze at it on the tree every year and thought it was so beautiful.

In 1982, glitter took on a whole new meaning for me. I made my first glitter greeting card and everyone loved it. I knew I had hit on something innovative but I wished I had glitter that was finer, that had more finesse and sophistication to it. I wanted to write calligraphy using glitter. I started researching and asking, "I want this ... can you do this?" Soon I had the glitter and adhesives made to my specifications.

I started by creating 21 card designs. I took them to five local alternative card stores. The very first store ordered several dozen cards. I was surprised and delighted.

I had no idea that this new glittering method of mine would lead to creating my own glitter colors. What an artist's dream! I started off with metallic glitter and I thought the colors were gorgeous. Then I moved on to opaque polyester glitter. I saw a brilliance I had never seen before. From there I created transparent colors that were influenced by flowers, inspired by my mother's career as a floral designer. Now I have several color combination kits for artists to choose from made by my company, Art Institute Glitter, Inc.

Glitter is my passion. It is dynamic. It spurs my creativity and gives me joy. It's instantaneously gratifying and beautiful. Even though there are already more than 375 colors in the Art Glitter line, I will continue to create unique glitter colors the rest of my days.

Barbara

Twenty years after I developed a passion for glitter, I'm still using it to dress up cards, tags, bags, and just about anything else that could use a little sparkle.

Table of Contents

CHAPTER 1

Introduction

You may be thinking, why use glitter? Isn't that a child's craft decoration, used on school projects and ornaments? That may be the only way it was used years ago, but today it is used in fine art, sophisticated crafting, the fabric industry, cosmetics, automotive, home decor, and nail products. Today it is applied to quilts, scrapbooks, polymer clay jewelry, silk flowers, costumes, decorations, cards, candles, soap, wrapping paper, fairies, and dolls. The list goes on and on. What has brought about this transformation? The availability of quality glitter in a myriad of sparkling colors, sizes, and types makes it a tool for all fields in the arts-and-crafts world.

To Glitter or Not to Glitter

From beginning to end, glitter adds excitement and adventure to everyday objects. It brings life to your projects. Glitter is instant creativity, instant beauty, and instant gratification. You can get as intricate or as simple as you want. Use glitter as your main focus or as a way to finish off your project by giving it an extra zing.

There is a variety of glitter types available for every occasion and a complete color palette to show off your work. You can use micro-fine glitter on a sophisticated art piece, ultra-fine glitter for just the right amount of sparkle, or you can choose chunky hologram glitter for a fun and funky look. Glitter complements other products such as glass plates, rhinestones, gold leafing, fusible film and fiber, metal findings, votive holders, wood signs, ribbon, fabric, and quilts. We are always discovering new ways to use it.

Throughout this book we take you through the world of glitter, revealing the different types, techniques, color varieties, and special effects. You will learn how to control glitter, choose the correct adhesive, and create diverse artistic projects, from small detail pieces to creations worthy of framing. Some projects use clip art included in the back of the book and others use stamps, printed fabric, or finished artwork. You will also learn advanced glitter shading, rainbow writing, spot glittering, how to enhance existing work, and all the different techniques that go along with stamping and paper arts. The cards, bags, and tags you make will take you beyond the average gift-giving experience, creating works of art that will be cherished for years to come.

Glitter, Tools & Techniques

Before starting a sparkling project, take the time to read over this chapter and familiarize yourself with glitter, its tools, and its fun techniques.

There are so many different techniques in achieving glitter artistry, but it mainly comes down to one common factor: control. Control is essential to attaining the effects you want. Using the right type of glitter for your project is the beginning of control.

The next component in gaining control is by means of adhesive. Adhesives all serve the same basic purpose: to adhere two elements together. By choosing the right type of adhesive and using the correct techniques you can achieve the results you want.

Glitter

Glitter Types

There are two major types of glitter: opaque and transparent.

Opaque glitter is jewel-toned and may be used on any background color of ink, paper, or fabric. Only use clear-drying adhesive and it will retain its original color.

Transparent glitter on the other hand is sheer and is influenced by any background color and/or adhesive. Therefore, if you use a transparent pink glitter on a blue background the resulting glitter color will appear purple.

Glitter Sizes

There are several sizes of glitter. These are the sizes we use most often.

Chunky glitter is four times larger than ultra-fine. Commonly used for areas of a project you really want to stand out.

Confetti glitter is the largest glitter used in this book. It is cut in random shapes about the size of a pencil eraser and is used to create specific background effects.

Micro-fine is a quarter the size of ultra-fine. It shimmers and has the look and feel of velvet. Used widely by artists and crafters alike on projects that call for less sparkle.

Ultra-fine, the size used most often in this book, is cut a quarter the size of craft glitter and gives off a beautiful sparkle. It is very versatile and can be used for calligraphy and detail work as well as large coverage areas.

Glitter Categories

The varying types of sheen and glitter colors available today have created new categories, including:

Hologram colors are a glitter color plus all the colors of the spectrum. Refracting light in a dazzling display of colors, hologram glitter can create a three-dimensional effect.

Neon colors are bright and festive. These colors really stand out and will super charge any project.

Pearlescent colors are more subtle, subdued colors. They have a beautiful pastel quality for a softer look.

Adhesives

Adhesive paper: Used frequently with glitter projects. Choose one that has a high-quality cardstock for the backing and a protective cover that peels away easily. All our projects start with a 8½" x 11" sheet. It is also available in 4¼" x 5½" sheets for cards and 12" x 12" sheets for larger projects and scrapbook pages.

Clear-drying adhesive: Used most commonly throughout this book. If an adhering agent is not mentioned in a direction, it is assumed to use clear-drying adhesive. We use a permanent industrial-strength adhesive that flows smoothly and dries acid-free, producing a clear finish when dry. It is important that your glue also dries flexible, otherwise it will crack, chip, and peel over time.

White-drying adhesive: Mainly used to give transparent and pearlescent glitters an opaque quality because it stays white. Never use with opaque glitters. Again, use an industrial-strength adhesive that flows and dries smoothly, and also stays permanently flexible. Experiment with your white-drying adhesive and get a feel for how it transforms transparent and pearlescent glitter colors.

Tools

Adhesive application machine: A non-electric appliance made to apply a smooth, non-repositionable layer of adhesive to paper element when rolled through a cartridge. Used to get an even layer of adhesive onto cardstock, mat board, glitter paper, etc.

Adhesive paper: 8½" x 11" or 12" x 12" sheets. Cardstock covered with a thin layer of adhesive on one side. Comes with protective cover that is peeled off when ready to use adhesive. Used to make a sheet of glitter paper, glitter lace paper, or as a stabilizer for fabric.

Baker's parchment paper: Heat-resistant paper used to protect surface of iron when heating fusible film and fiber.

Brush markers: Also known as watercolor markers. A permanent marker with a brush tip used for shading and coloring in images.

Cardstock: Paper that is a heavier weight than most stationery and decorative papers. Used for main body of a card and backgrounds for various art projects and scrapbooking.

Clear-drying adhesive: Industrial-strength adhesive for glitter, paper, cardboard, cardstock, transparencies, glass, plastic, wood, metal, and ceramics. When dry, the adhesive will be clear and flexible. Used for almost all projects as an application agent for glitter and for adhering two elements together.

Cloth: Cotton swatch used to keep stainless-steel pin and ultra-fine metal tip clean while using adhesive.

Decorative paper: Or scrapbook paper, comes in a range of sizes from 8" x 8" to 12" x 12" sheets. Paper that has images or designs in all colors. Used for background paper and as foreground images to apply glitter to.

Decorative scissors: Scissors with a decorative edge instead of a straight one. Used to cut decorative edges on paper, cardstock, and decorative paper.

Decoupage glue: A thick, clear-drying adhesive that creates a protective layer to objects when applied on top. Used to protect delicate items and keep several layers of a project together.

Double-sided tape: Roll that comes in several widths. We generally use ⅛" and ¼" sizes. Has a protective peel-off plastic liner. Used for making a strip of glitter and to mount two surfaces together.

Dryer sheet: Fibrous cloth with laundry softener on it. Used to rub on cardstock, glitter spoons, and trays to reduce static.

Embossing ink: Clear, sticky ink used with embossing powder sprinkled on top. Used to create a dimensional design or line with stamped art (**A**).

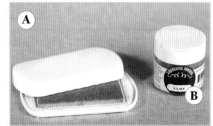

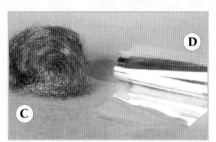

Embossing powder: A powder sprinkled on top of a stamped image using an inkpad or embossing ink. A heat tool is used to melt the powder to form a raised line (**B**).

Freezer paper: Heat-resistant paper coated with shiny plastic on one side. Used as a protective coating to resist glue or stiffener when ironed onto fabric.

Fusible fiber: Transparent fiber that fuses to itself with heat application. Make stamp impressions by placing on a stamp and heating with an iron or heat tool. Fuses with fusible film also (**C**).

Fusible film: Transparent film that fuses to itself with heat application. Make stamp impressions by placing on a stamp and heating with an iron. Fuses with fusible fiber also (**D**).

Fusible web: An iron-on web used to adhere fabric to other surfaces.

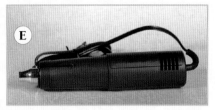

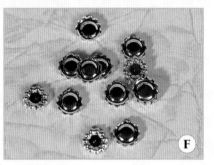

Glass glitter: Glitter made from glass. With time colors fade, making it a good product for vintage projects.

Heat tool: A hand-held electrical appliance that blows very hot air. Used to melt materials like embossing powder, fusible film, and fiber or to dry permanent and pigment ink (**E**).

Hole punch: A hand-held tool that makes holes in paper and cardstock. Comes in several shapes and sizes according to hole's circumference. Used to cut holes in tags.

Hot glue gun: An electrical appliance that heats glue (in the form of a glue stick) to be squeezed out the metal tip of "gun." Used on projects that need a fast-drying, flexible bond.

Inkpad, dye-based: Comes in several colors. Does not need to be dried with heat tool. Use this type of inkpad unless noted.

Inkpad, permanent: A soft pad containing ink that dries permanently. Used for most stamping projects and to color edges of paper.

Inkpad, pigment: A soft pad containing ink that stays slick and does not heat cure. Used to hold embossing powder onto project surface before heating.

Iron: Any size of iron with a non-stick coating used to bond fusible film and fiber. Projects use a dry, medium-high heat setting.

Ironing cloth: A treated cloth with a non-stick surface. Used as a protective barrier between iron and fusible film and fiber.

Jewelry casings: Round metal casings that jewels are set into. Used as decorative embellishments (**F**).

Leafing adhesive: Adhesive designed for three-dimensional free-hand leafing. Leafing is applied after adhesive has dried (**G**).

Light table: Electrical appliance that encloses a light inside a box with a milky glass cover for tracing clip art onto paper.

Masking tape: Inexpensive tape on a roll used to tack two surfaces together.

Mat board: A thick, colored board used as a stabilizing background or as a protective mat to cut on.

Mat knife: A tool with a pointed blade on one end. Used with a ruler to cut straight lines.

Metal leafing: Imitation gold leaf. Comes in thin sheets or rolls with backing. Apply pressure to adhere to adhesive tape or leaf adhesive. Used to create a metallic look, usually gold (**H**).

Mounting dots: Round, three-dimensional foam dots with adhesive on both sides. Comes in several sizes. Used to raise a subject off the surface of a project.

Noodger: A small rectangle cut from cardstock for correcting glue and glitter mistakes by pushing a wild line back in place or removing a wet, glittered dot.

Paintbrush: Small, soft paintbush of any kind. Used to brush on adhesive and to brush away leafing after it has been applied.

Permanent marker: Black permanent ink marker that won't smudge or smear. Used to darken the edges of projects.

Polyester lace: Assorted 5" x 7" patterns used as stencils. The more open the design the more the result will resemble lace. Used with adhesive paper to create glitter lace paper (**I**).

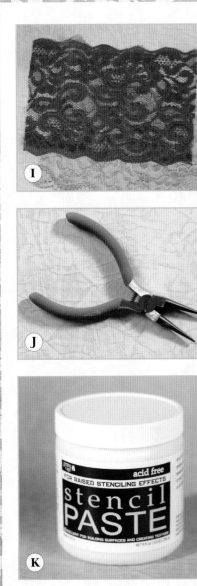

Repositionable tape: Tape designed to tack two surfaces together temporarily and then move to another spot without tearing surfaces.

Round needle-nose pliers: Wire-cutting and bending tool used to make bug antenna in V-shape or rounded shape (**J**).

Rubber stamps: Raised rubber surface made into an image, design, or letters. All stamps in this book are listed as rubber stamps but for most projects you can use acrylic and unmounted stamps. However, when imprinting a stamp image onto fusible fiber or film, stamp must be mounted. Used with an inkpad to create instant images and designs.

Spoon: Plastic, silver, or metal spoons are acceptable. Used for sprinkling glitter onto adhesive. Choose one with a slightly pointed tip and a deep bowl.

Stainless-steel pin: Place through the opening of the ultra-fine metal tip to store bottle and keep opening clear.

Stencil paste: A paste you use with stencils to create a raised effect. Used to create a three-dimensional effect on most surfaces (**K**).

Stencils: A thick plastic sheet with perforated shapes you can transfer onto paper. Used to make ovals around an image or to draw perfect circles.

Three-dimensional embossing adhesive: Three-dimensional embossing emulsion used with traditionally pre-embossed stamped art and embossing powders. Heat tool is used after emulsion has dried. Use to create a raised, free-hand embossed effect (**L**).

Transfer paper: Carbon paper used to transfer an image onto another piece of paper when placed in between the two.

Transparency sheet: Acetate sheet used as a clear surface to stamp on, draw on, and/or apply glitter to.

Trays: Plastic disposable trays, creased papers, and coffee filters are all used for keeping glitter colors separate and to catch excess glitter as it is tapped off project.

Ultra-fine metal tip: Created to screw onto adhesive bottle for applying adhesive in fine, controlled lines or dots. Used to fill in small areas in a stamp design or other artwork for precision with detailing.

Wax-tipped tool: Small sticks with a waxy end used for applying small findings that are hard to pick up with fingers.

White-drying adhesive: An industrial-strength adhesive for transparent or pearlescent glitter only, never opaque glitter. When dry, the adhesive will remain white. Used mainly for creating a snow effect with crystal glitter.

Techniques

Basic Glitter Application Techniques

The basic way to apply glitter to most surfaces is as follows:

1. Put glitter in tray.
2. Attach metal tip to adhesive bottle.
3. Squeeze out line of glue.
4. Spoon on glitter over glue line.
5. Tap off excess glitter back into tray.
6. Fix mistakes and keep tools clean with pin, noodger, and cloth.

Sounds simple? Well it is, but there are many techniques involved to create the effects you want in becoming a glitter artist. Let's look at each step closer.

Putting Glitter into Tray

A little bit of glitter goes a long way, so you can purchase a small amount if you want. However, in order to work quickly and smoothly, try to use ½ ounce of each color.

Your tray can be a disposable plastic tray with an opening of at least 2" x 2" to give yourself enough space to catch excess glitter as you tap it off your project. An option to trays is to place a creased 8½" x 11" piece of paper under glitter jar. A crease down the middle of your paper allows you to pour excess glitter back into jar.

Another option to trays would be to use a pleated coffee filter with a flat bottom. Place one of these under each glitter jar. Then use the crease between two pleats to pour glitter back into jar when finished.

Attaching Metal Tip to Adhesive Bottle

Your new adhesive bottle comes sealed with a cap. Remove cap and peel off seal. Attach spout by twisting on top of bottle to the right. When tight, give it one more turn. Attach metal tip to spout with downward motion, turning it to the right. Again, when tight, give it one more turn. If glue seeps out of either of these places when pressure is applied, give it another turn.

Squeezing Out Line of Glue

Hold glue bottle in your hand like a pencil resting on the knuckle of the middle finger. Only your thumb applies the pressure. Don't squeeze from both sides.

Touch metal tip to paper surface before applying any pressure; this will ensure control of adhesive. If you squeeze the glue bottle before touching the surface, you will be unsure of your glue placement. Apply a small amount of pressure and glide glue bottle across paper to make a line. While applying glue to most projects don't be stingy; lay it on generously.

Spooning Glitter on Glue Line

Spoon on glitter while adhesive is wet, white, and shiny. If surface of adhesive starts to get a skin on it before applying glitter, let it dry completely and apply fresh glue on top. Any kind of spoon will do, but one that is slightly pointed with a deep bowl works best. While holding paper in one hand, dip spoon in glitter with other hand and hold it over glue line. With a slight twist of your wrist, allow glitter to fall off tip of spoon and cover all sides of adhesive.

Tapping Off Excess Glitter

Tip paper over tray and let excess glitter slide off into tray. Continue turning paper until upside down over tray and tap the back of it with your spoon, shedding even more glitter. Glue will not fall off, nor will glitter. Adhesive is industrial strength and really grabs the glitter.

Fixing Mistakes & Keeping Tools Clean

Stainless Steel Pin

For short periods of time you can store your adhesive bottle with the metal tip on by placing a stainless-steel pin inside the spout. It is important that the pin be stainless steel; any other pin will rust and discolor the adhesive. Also use the pin for cleaning out dried adhesive.

If you apply the wrong color of glitter or realize that the surface of adhesive has started to dry after applying glitter, stir the glue and glitter. Apply more glitter (and glue if desired) or change glitter to the color you wanted it to be originally.

Noodger

If you have made a mistake with your glue, apply glitter first. Flex noodger between your thumb and first two fingers. Place edge on paper then slide it at an angle up against glue and push your mistake back into place. You can even wipe away a whole section of glue with glitter on it.

Noodgers are great for making lines straight, separating glue areas, wiping off dots, and even for dipping into large drops of glue to scoop out excess. It is important to always apply glitter to glue before noodging it. This keeps glue from spreading back to its original place.

Cloth

Use a cotton cloth to wipe your metal tip frequently. This will ensure a clean, controlled application of adhesive. Also use it to wipe off noodger. Paper towels are not recommended because they leave small fibers behind.

Essential Techniques

In addition to the basic glitter application techniques there are some fundamental techniques discussed in detail below that are essential to becoming a glitter artist:

Outlining

Outlining with glitter is the same as outlining with a pencil, pen, etc.; you are tracing over an existing image. Take an image like a stamp, print, or sticker, and trace over its lines with clear-drying adhesive. Then sprinkle on its coordinating color, matching the colors beneath as closely as possible.

Freehand

Applying glitter by the freehand method is the exact opposite of outlining. Instead of working with an existing image, you draw the image, line, or word in adhesive. Then sprinkle on any color of glitter you desire. You can layer your glitter colors before letting the project dry between each color. For example: Write a name with adhesive (**A**) and cover glue with one color (**B**).

Draw confetti dropping down through the name by dragging tip of adhesive through glittered name (**C**) or add a star that breaks through the curl of a "Y." Cover with another color of glitter (**D**).

The name keeps its shape because the adhesive grabs onto the glitter, preventing the new adhesive from smearing the old (**E**). This technique is best performed with only opaque colors because they are less likely to pollute, or run into, each other.

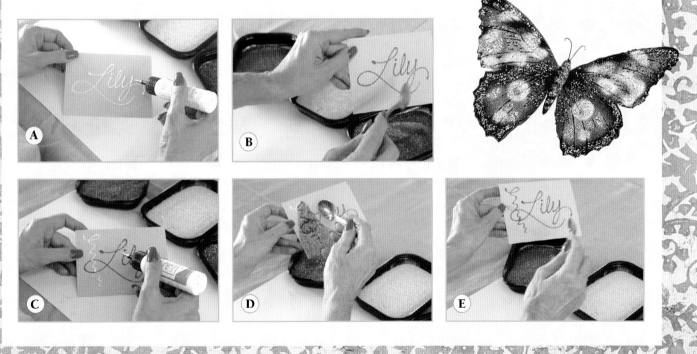

Spot Glittering

If you have several small areas of glue to cover with different colors of glitter, like stars, you don't have to draw and add glitter to each one separately; you can spot glitter several at one time.

First draw 4 or 5 stars with adhesive randomly on paper (F). Take the star that is closest to an edge and hold it over one color. Load your spoon with a small amount of glitter; let it start to fall off the tip of your spoon and onto the paper about an inch in front of star (G).

While twisting your wrist slightly, glide your spoon towards star, continuing to let glitter fall until it is covered (H). Tap off excess glitter away from the rest of the stars (I). Continue covering other stars in same manner, changing colors for each one (J). Make sure you get glitter on the glue before it starts to dry (K).

As you get better at this technique you can spot glitter shapes that are closer together or even touching each other. Just start with one color on the end of a line, tap excess off, then come up to it, without necessarily going over it with another color.

As you become faster, approach the glue with your spoon in one hand, letting the glitter fall towards the glue, twisting your wrist towards the paper. At the same time twist your paper towards your glitter, allowing the glitter to cover your adhesive and fall off your paper in one swift move. Keep twisting your wrist to apply glitter and let it fall off paper, away from the rest of your project until done.

Shading

You can shade beautifully with glitter, making colors gradually flow into each other minus the stark lines between. Transparent colors work best for this technique.

For example: Shade a flower and leaves by starting with the center of your image and working your way out.

Fill in center of flower with glue and bright yellow glitter. Place several tiny dots of glue in the center of flower to form stamens. Flood with a dark orange glitter. Apply a thin line of glue on the "turned-back" petals. Cover with a bright yellow glitter of your choice.

Completely fill in one petal with glue. Turn the paper so the center of the flower is nearest your spoon. Sprinkle inside of petal nearest the center of the flower with a dark orange glitter, using very little glitter and tapping it gently off the tip of the spoon. Tap off excess glitter from glue work.

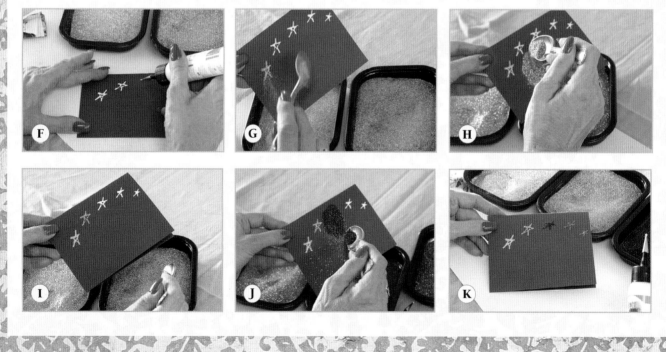

Turn paper around so edge of flower is nearest your spoon, and lightly dust just the edge of the petal with bright yellow, using very little glitter and tapping it gently off the tip of the spoon. Tap off excess glitter, away from glue work. Flood entire petal with bright orange glitter. Repeat for all petals.

To shade a leaf, fill entire leaf with glue, remembering where the large center vein runs. Pick up dark green glitter with the side of the spoon so that a thin line of glitter lays in the spoon's edge. Carefully position spoon over leaf and tap off a small amount of glitter in a line from the side of the spoon to form the vein.

Sprinkle a light green glitter over the leaf, towards the center of the leaf, off the tip of the spoon, forming highlights. Sprinkle a bright green glitter over entire leaf.

Brushing on Adhesive

Some projects call for a very thin layer of glitter. The adhesive we use straight from the bottle is a three-dimensional adhesive and too thick for this purpose. Thin this adhesive a little by placing a small amount in a container and combine with about 30 percent water. Brush diluted adhesive onto any project surface and sprinkle with glitter. Be sure to work in small areas. Since adhesive is thin, it will dry quickly.

Advanced Techniques

Rainbow Glittering

The rainbow glittering technique uses the spot glittering method to create a rainbow of colors across an image or word.

First, place your glitter trays in a row, like a rainbow. Use either all opaque or transparent colors; don't mix types. Then draw or trace over one image or word in adhesive (**A**). Load your spoon with a small amount of glitter. Let it start to fall off the tip of your spoon onto the paper about an inch in front of your image or word (**B**).

While twisting your wrist slightly, glide your spoon towards the beginning of the image, continuing to let glitter fall, creating a line of glitter that connects with adhesive (**C**). Tap off excess glitter away from the rest of the image.

Bright Idea

Positioning Spoon and Sprinkling Glitter

You are not covering your adhesive, only allowing a little bit of dark glitter to slide off the tip of your spoon towards the dark side or shadow of a shape. Then switch to a lighter color to sprinkle over the highlights. Next cover the rest of your adhesive with a bright color for the body of an image, all the while turning your paper around so that the area you are working on is closest to your spoon, then tapping excess glitter away from rest of the adhesive. Also, hold your spoon about 1½" above adhesive. This gives the glitter time to float down and "dust" your shape instead of forming a line.

Continue to cover the adhesive, one color at a time down the line of rainbow colors, applying glitter in stripes, lightly overlapping (**D, E**). Tap off between each color change (**F**). Let image dry (**G**).

To Make Glitter Lace

Once you've done this technique you will begin to look at your old scraps of lace in a totally different light, saving everything that has a pattern to it. You can make glitter lace as large as 12" x 12"; generally a quarter

of a sheet (4¼" x 5½") will do. For this example we will use:

Glitter
- Ultra-fine opaque glitter: medium purple, pink
- Ultra-fine transparent glitter: light blue, pale pink, pale yellow

Materials
- 5" x 7" piece of lace
- Adhesive paper

Instructions
Cut adhesive paper to 4¼" x 5½". Remove backing from adhesive paper and position lace on sticky side of paper (**A**). Press down and smooth lace firmly onto adhesive paper (**B**).

Make sure that all parts of lace are firmly in contact with adhesive paper. If there is a gap, opaque glitter will flood that area.

Randomly sprinkle glitter over entire surface of lace attached to

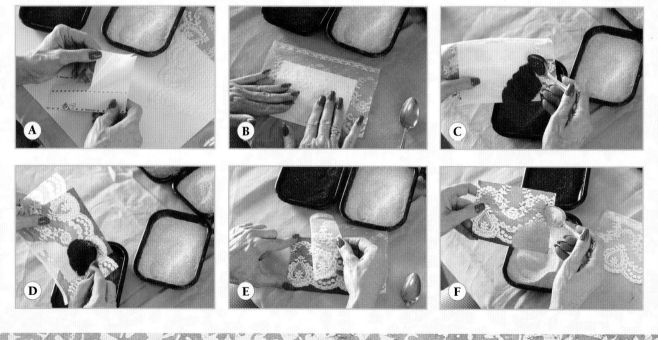

adhesive paper (**C**). Tap glitter off after each application (**D**).

Pull off lace to reveal lace pattern (**E**). Flood remaining surface with glitter in random pattern, making sure paper is covered with glitter (**F**).

Putting Glitter on Transparencies

Stamp image on transparency with black permanent inkpad. (Do not use a pigment inkpad; ink will not stay fixed.) Dry lightly with heat tool until ink has turned from shiny to matte. You can also transfer images onto transparency by tracing with fine black permanent ink pen or by copying it with dry toner or laser copier. If you use a copier, make sure you have the right type of transparency for your machine. Keep these tips in mind when applying glitter and you will have stunning results every time:

- Approach transparency from the side it is stamped on.
- Use only clear-drying adhesive to apply glitter.
- Transparent glitters let the sun shine through, but opaque colors are just as elegant.
- As adhesive has a tendency to move away from walls of image, be sure to bump up right to the edges and use generously.
- Leave some areas "un-glittered" to let background show through.

- Hold transparency up to a light to see if you've missed any spots.
- It usually takes overnight for a transparency to completely dry.
- Project is dry when the smooth side reveals glitter only, no white glue.
- The front side is generally the smooth side, but the back side is just as brilliant.

Other Stamping and Embellishment Techniques

Basic Stamping

Basic stamping is pretty simple. Take a stamp image and pat it firmly onto inkpad surface.

Position inked stamp above area to be stamped and place it firmly onto surface. Hold stamp in place for 2–5 seconds with minimal pressure. Lift stamp off surface without smearing ink.

Most dye-based inks only take a few seconds to dry. Heat surface of permanent ink with a heat tool to set ink into surface.

Embossing

Embossing creates a raised effect on your stamped image. You can stamp your image with clear embossing ink or pigmented ink (**A**) then cover ink with embossing powder (**B**). Tap off excess powder (**C**).

If there are a few grains of powder left on un-inked surface, carefully wipe them away with a brush.

Wave a heat tool over powder until melted together, forming a hard surface (**D**).

You can also apply embossing powders to adhesive tape or paper; heat to create a bubbly, raised texture.

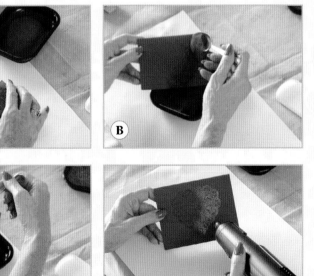

Fusible Film

You can easily make images on fusible film with ink, a stamp, and an iron. First, ink rubber stamp with black permanent ink (**A**). Lay the stamp, rubber-side up, on table.

Carefully set four sheets of film on surface of inked stamp (**B**). Without moving film, cover film with baker's parchment paper or ironing cloth (**C**). Press (not iron), entire surface of stamp for 5-10 seconds with hot iron (**D**). Peel off fused film. Cut off excess or leave intact to add glitter to (**E**). Cut out image closely with scissors.

Fusible Fiber

Fusible fiber is a lot like fusible film only cut in strands. Carefully set a small portion of fiber on surface of inked stamp (**F**). It may help to roll fiber in your hands and form a ball to position on top of stamp. Without moving fiber, cover it with baker's parchment paper or ironing cloth (**G**). Press (not iron), entire surface of stamp for 5-10 seconds with hot iron (**H**). Peel off fused film (**I**).

Leafing

Leafing can be applied to leafing adhesive or double-sided adhesive tape to create a faux metal effect. It comes in sheets or rolls with a backing.

Lay down your leafing adhesive or double-sided adhesive tape first. If using leafing adhesive it's best to apply leafing compound just after it turns clear. It may have a little "white" on the inside. The adhesive needs to be almost dry but still tacky to the touch. If you wait too long, until it is very clear, it may not stick as well.

Lay leafing, metal side down, on top of adhesive and pat it into place. Lightly brush off excess leaf with a paintbrush.

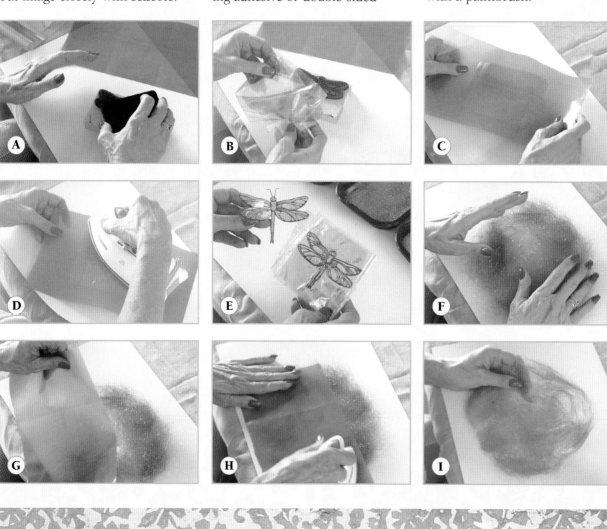

Three-Dimensional Embossing

Three-dimensional embossing uses glue with embossing powders to make a three-dimensional embossed effect. Start with stamped or embossed image then outline highlights or fill in areas you want to draw attention to with three-dimensional embossing adhesive. Cover glue with embossing powders and let it completely dry overnight.

Wave heat tool over three-dimensional embossed area. Start to heat it from underneath and warm up whole area. You don't want to burn the powders that are sitting on top of the adhesive. Once it has warmed up underneath you can finish on top. Since it is three-dimensional it takes a little longer to heat than conventional embossing.

Use your three-dimensional embossing adhesive like a pencil as well. Create freehand designs or write out names with adhesive then emboss.

Transferring an Image

There are numerous clip art images available in the Clip Art section (pages 113-121). To transfer them onto adhesive paper, cardstock, or paper use one of these techniques:

Light Table

Photocopy image onto white paper. Place photocopied image on light table and tack down with masking tape. Place paper or light-colored cardstock (as long as cardstock is not too thick or dark) on top and tack down also.

Turn light on and, depending on how permanent your image needs to be, trace image with a pencil or black felt-tip marker. This method can also be used with sunlight coming through a window. Tape photocopied image and paper onto clean window to trace.

Transfer Paper

Transfer paper or carbon paper is your best method for transferring an image onto cardstock, mat board, or papers that are too dark to see through.

Lay your project surface down first. Cover with transfer paper and position photocopied image on top. Secure edges with masking tape. Press firmly with a pencil or pen over image lines. Save transfer paper for future projects.

You can make your own transfer paper by covering one side of a blank sheet of paper with white chalk (for transferring onto a dark surface), dark chalk, carbon, or charcoal stick.

After transferring image you will need to go over image again with a pencil then brush off chalk residue.

Bright Idea

Variations with Film and Fiber

Once heat is applied you'll notice the color will change. Experiment with using different colors of film and fiber together and see what you come up with. Also experiment with the amount of press time you use. The longer it is heated the more color loss will occur, leaving a coppery tone. Film and fiber will even begin to burn and bubble if heated too long. A great trick is to take your stamped film and/or fiber image, hold the edges over a candle flame, and char the edges.

Bright Idea

Avoid Smearing Stamped Image

It is very important not to move the first layer of film around once it has made contact with the inked stamp. If the ink smears, try to wipe off, let it dry, and start again. When pressing with the iron, try not to move the iron around on top of the film. This also helps prevent smearing of the image.

CHAPTER 2

Travel & Vintage Inspired

Heart-felt memories are to be treasured. They enrich our lives. They bind us together and expand our sense of time. For a hundred years, glitter has added something special to a cherished card. Glitter brings attention to everything it touches. It does not have to be loud and gaudy. It can be subtle and tasteful. Subdued transparent antique rose-toned glitter colors blend beautifully with sepia backgrounds, while a jewel-toned opaque antique gold glitter adds just the right amount of richness to a red velvet hue. Glitter connects the past with the present. In the past, our Victorian ancestors only had a few colors of glass glitter to work with. Today, we have multiple polyester colors to choose from that are equally successful. We use them to outline the reproduction of a vintage seed packet label or to accent an embossed picture frame. With bits and pieces of our past and all that we are in the present, we bring what was theirs with what is ours to the same table. This chapter highlights various ways to showcase your journeys and memories of long ago with sophistication and charm.

Vintage Label Card

Glitter

- Ultra-fine transparent glitter: choose five colors that match vintage print's light and dark green in leaves, light and dark colors of flowers, and light yellow for stamens

Materials

- ⅛" double-sided tape
- Adhesive application machine
- Cardstock in two colors: one contrasting color of vintage print for mat, another contrasting color for card
- Clear-drying adhesive with ultra-fine tip attached
- Reproduction print of vintage floral, seed pack, or other old label
- Scissors
- Spoon

Bright Idea
Getting Out the Wrinkles

If an adhesive application machine is not available, squeeze your glue bottle lightly, creating thin lines of adhesive across the cardstock. You can even smudge glue with your finger to spread it into a thin layer. This will alleviate glue bumps that can wrinkle your cardstock. It also helps to stack books on top of the cardstock while it is drying.

Instructions

1. Cut border cardstock ⅛" larger around than vintage print.

2. Glue print to mat and weight down or run print through adhesive application machine and mount in center of mat.

3. Fold other cardstock and cut ½" larger than matted print. Glue matted print to front of folded cardstock, leaving ¼" border around all sides.

4. Glue and sprinkle glitter on stamens (flower centers) with light yellow color. Make color change and add dark flower glitter color to area surrounding stamens. Repeat with petal edges using light flower glitter color.

5. Let card dry five minutes under heat of lamp between color changes or keep one color from falling on top of another color when spooning on glitter to avoid "color pollution."

6. Apply glue to dark edges of a few leaves at a time. Glitter in dark green. Finish edges in light green. Add some light green glitter where light catches surface of leaves.

7. Glitter small pattern in flower pot, working in small areas at a time. *Hint:* You want to get the glitter on the glue while it is wet, white, and shiny.

8. For the old label card, apply double-sided tape on top of border around print; remove plastic guard. Sprinkle on light yellow glitter.

Recycled Gift Bag

Glitter

- Ultra-fine opaque glitter: avocado, brown, dark copper, light copper
- Ultra-fine transparent glitter: flax

Materials

- 4" x 5" piece of lace
- 4¼" x 5½" adhesive paper
- Brown paper bag
- Buttons: green, flat, 6
- Cardstock: light beige
- Clear-drying adhesive with ultra-fine metal tip attached
- Decorative-edge scissors
- Embossing inkpad
- Embossing powder: copper
- Heat tool
- Inkpads: brown, ochre, sage
- Pencil
- Rubber stamps: assorted postage, Congratulations, or other appropriate word stamp
- Scissors
- Spoon
- Stencil: oval

Instructions

To Make Glitter Lace Oval

1. Pull backing off adhesive paper. Hold lace in U-shape, touching center of lace to center of adhesive paper. Let sides float down. Press and smooth lace firmly in place with fingers.

2. Spoon on avocado glitter in small area of lace then tap off excess downwards across area just glittered, avoiding contact with remaining sticky surface. Continue spooning on dark copper and brown glitter in same manner until adhesive paper is covered. Peel off lace to reveal lace pattern. Fill in remaining white adhesive paper with flax glitter.

3. Using stencil, draw oval on back of glitter lace and cut out oval. Set aside.

To Make Background

1. Cut cardstock to 5½" x 8½". Stamp with assorted postage images using all three inkpads. Cut stamped cardstock in rectangle to fit over store logo that may be on front and back of bag. Cut all corners off cardstock with decorative-edge scissors.

2. Cut long, narrow strip of remaining stamped cardstock to cover secondary logo. Ink all sides of cardstock strip by sliding them across brown inkpad.

Embellishing Store Bag

1. Adhere finished cardstock pieces onto bag with adhesive, covering store logos. Attach glitter lace oval to center of larger rectangular cardstock with adhesive. Outline outside edges of cardstock with adhesive and sprinkle with light copper glitter. Outline around outside of lace oval with equally spaced glue dots and sprinkle on avocado glitter.

2. Stamp Congratulations or other word on lower strip of cardstock using embossing inkpad. Spoon on copper embossing powder over word and tap off excess powder. Wave heat tool over word until powder melts into a solid.

3. Using clear-drying adhesive, glue one green button in all four corners of rectangle cardstock. Glue two remaining green buttons on either side of word.

Congratulations

Faux Rhinestones & Pearls Card

Glitter

- Chunky hologram glitter: jet eye
- Ultra-fine hologram glitter: black hole, nebula
- Ultra-fine pearlescent glitter: pearl white

Materials

- Cardstock: black, light gray tweed
- Clear-drying adhesive with ultra-fine metal tip attached
- Scissors
- Spoon
- Victorian design (included in Clip Art section, pages 113-121)
- White-drying adhesive with ultra-fine metal tip attached

Bright Idea

Using Adhesive Application Machine

If you have an adhesive application machine, run the gray cardstock through it, peel off the backing, and adhere it to the black cardstock. This will give you a nice, flat surface between each cardstock. Adhesive application machines are also wonderful for eliminating drying time and fussing with books to help flatten the surface.

Instructions

1. Photocopy Victorian design onto gray tweed cardstock. Outline, a little at a time, all stems and leaves in tiny dots with clear-drying adhesive. Sprinkle on black hole hologram glitter.

2. Dot center line in leaf and trace veins with light clear-drying adhesive application. Sprinkle on black hole hologram glitter as you go.

3. Add dots to left side of leaf and sprinkle with nebula hologram glitter. Dot between black hole dots of veins and sprinkle on jet eye hologram glitter. *Optional:* Extra dots can be added at the tips of the leaves and sprinkled black.

4. On centers of largest flowers, apply clear-drying adhesive then sprinkle on jet eye hologram glitter. Apply white-drying adhesive on flower petals then sprinkle on pearl white glitter. Let glue dry 10 minutes.

5. On smaller flowers, apply clear-drying adhesive then sprinkle on black hole glitter at center and jet eye glitter on petals.

6. On rectangular border, apply evenly spaced adhesive dots and sprinkle on nebula glitter. Glue and sprinkle glitter as you go. Let dry 1 hour.

7. Trim gray tweed cardstock to size of image, leaving ¼" border around perimeter. Cut and fold black cardstock to 5½" x 4" top-fold card.

8. Lightly glue back and corners of gray cardstock. Place gray cardstock onto black cardstock, ¼" away from folded edge. Trim any excess black cardstock to leave an even ¼" border all the way around.

9. Open card up flat and weight with books while drying.

Vintage Tags on a Tag

Glitter

- Micro-fine opaque glitter: black, gold

Materials

- 3" x 5" vintage or reproduction paper with handwriting on it
- 4¼" x 5½" adhesive paper
- 5" x 7" piece of polyester lace in small, fine pattern
- 5" x 7" piece of tulle netting
- Cardstock: tan
- Clear-drying adhesive with ultra-fine metal tip attached
- Embossing inkpad
- Embossing powder: black, copper, gold
- Heat tool
- Inkpads: black, brown
- Rubber stamps: small spiral icon, vintage square
- Scissors
- String: brown
- Tag: miniature, on a string
- Walnut-stained tags: extra small, large, medium, small, 1 each
- Watch parts: assorted tiny pieces, including face

Instructions

1. Rip vintage paper to fit inside borders of large tag. Ink sides of tags and ripped paper by running edges across surface of brown inkpad.

2. Glue torn paper onto largest tag, then medium tag onto middle of torn paper.

3. Cut adhesive paper in half. To make glitter lace paper using tulle, take one section of adhesive paper and firmly smooth netting onto its surface. Flood surface with black glitter and tap off. Gently pull off netting and apply gold glitter to fill in sticky, white pattern. Rip small piece out of lace paper in irregular shape and ink edges in brown. Glue onto medium tag, overlapping torn paper.

4. Stamp vintage square design with black ink onto tan cardstock. Cut out and ink edges in brown. Glue stamped image and small tag onto glittered lace paper and medium tag.

5. Make piece of embossed lace paper using same glitter lace technique, using embossing powder instead. Press lace onto other half of adhesive paper, coat with copper embossing powder, remove lace, and coat with gold embossing powder. Melt powders with heat tool.

6. Rip irregularly shaped piece of embossed lace, ink edges in brown, and glue to center of small tag.

7. Rip irregularly shaped piece of embossed lace, brown edges with ink, and glue embossed lace to center of small tag.

8. Stamp spiral icon image onto extra-small tag using embossing inkpad and sprinkle on black embossing powder. Melt powder with heat tool. Ink edges with brown inkpad and loop string through hole. Glue onto top of embossed lace paper inside small tag.

9. Weight collage with books and let dry for several hours. After everything is dry and flattened, outline with adhesive and sprinkle gold glitter inside lines of spirals, gold dots on glitter netting paper, and black dots on tags.

10. Outline vintage square stamp in black glitter dots and accent with gold glitter.

11. Tie string of miniature tag through hole of largest tag. Glue on watch parts with adhesive.

Travel Collage Tag Book

Note: Since this is a collage project, leftover scraps of fabric, paper, ribbon, and other two-dimensional pieces from other projects can easily be incorporated into these tags.

Glitter

• Assorted ultra-fine and micro-fine glitter in opaque and transparent colors to match chosen color palette (include black and diva gold)

Materials

• ¼" double-sided tape
• Brush marker: brown
• Clear-drying adhesive with ultra-fine metal tip attached
• Decorative fabric
• Embossing powder: gold
• Heat tool
• Mat board: tan
• Rubber stamp: frame
• Scissors
• Spoon
• Tag book with approximately 10 pages

Instructions

1. Cut decorative fabric to ⅛" smaller than front and back cover of tag book. Glue onto tag book and weight down with books.

2. Apply double-sided tape to edge (it should overlap edges of fabric); remove plastic guard. Sprinkle on gold glitter.

3. Using brown brush marker, color cardboard between binding rings and thick edges of cover.

4. Add glue dots then sprinkle on ultra-fine or micro-fine glitter in colors that match fabric between binding rings on front and back covers. Sprinkle glitter around circle openings that strings go through.

5. Emboss frame stamp on tan mat board using gold embossing powder and heat tool. Cut to size of stamp.

6. Using embossed design as guide, glue and sprinkle glitter on one side of frame at a time. An easy choice is to use glitter in same color as embossing powder. Let dry 10 minutes. Add black (or any other color of glitter) as accent. Let dry.

7. To put title inside gilded frame, you have a few options: write in adhesive and sprinkle with matching glitter color, emboss with word stamp, or use sticker lettering on piece of cardstock trimmed to fit into center of frame. Let dry if using glue. Glue title into frame; glue frame to center of front cover.

8. Keep adding to each page until it feels finished, but be careful not to overdo it. How much you embellish is based on personal preference.

Pressed Flowers Card

Glitter

- Micro-fine opaque glitter: diva gold, purple morpho
- Micro-fine transparent glitter: fawn

Materials

- ¼" double-sided tape
- 4¼" x 5½" adhesive paper
- 5" x 7" piece of polyester lace
- Cardstock: tan and complementary color of flowers
- Clear acrylic sealer spray
- Clear-drying adhesive with ultra-fine metal tip attached
- Decorative-edge scissors
- Dried and pressed pansies in different sizes and colors or flowers cut from wrapping paper or napkins, 8-9
- Scissors

Instructions

1. To make glitter lace with pansies on adhesive paper, remove backing from adhesive paper. Carefully place pansies on sticky surface.

2. Lay lace on top of pansies and adhesive paper. Hold lace in U-shape, touching center of lace to center of adhesive paper. Let sides float down. Press and smooth lace firmly in place with fingers. Pay special attention to pressing lace around pansy edges. Lace needs to have firm contact with adhesive paper for pattern of lace to be crisp and distinct.

3. Sprinkle entire surface with purple morpho glitter. Peel off lace to reveal lace pattern. Fill in remaining white adhesive paper with fawn glitter

4. Cut and fold tan cardstock to 5½" x 4¼" top-fold card. Run thin glue line across top front edge of cardstock. Place glitter lace paper onto card, raising it up ¼" from bottom. Turn card over and apply glue to glitter lace overhang. Press onto back of card.

5. On front bottom edge of card, cut off ¼" of glitter lace paper (including cardstock) with decorative-edge scissors. With thin line, glue lace paper to flap of cardstock.

6. Apply thin line of adhesive then sprinkle on purple morpho glitter to bottom edge of flap, following cut of decorative edge.

7. Make glue dots inside centers of all pansies and sprinkle with diva gold glitter. On inside bottom edge, apply double-sided tape, remove plastic guard, then sprinkle on diva gold glitter. *Optional:* You may glue down cut-off glitter lace strip and decorate edge in purple or gold glitter instead.

8. Spray entire card with clear acrylic sealer. Let dry completely.

Antique Photo Tag

Glitter

- Micro-fine opaque glitter: black or brown, diva gold
- Micro-fine transparent glitter: fawn or off-white

Materials

- ⅛" double-sided tape
- ¾"-wide decorative ribbon: sheer black rayon with embroidered vine design
- 1½" x 2" copy of 1890s photo
- 4" x 5" handmade paper: off-white
- Bead trim: in gold, brown, and black tones, with black edging
- Cardstock: tan
- Clear-drying adhesive with ultra-fine metal tip attached
- Hole punch
- Inkpads: brown, tan
- Rubber stamp: fern leaf
- Scissors
- String
- Tag: large, walnut stained

Instructions

1. Ink all sides of tag by running edges across brown inkpad; let dry.

2. Cut ribbon to fit top of tag. Apply adhesive to top of tag and attach ribbon. When adhesive is dry, trim corners and hole punch ribbon over tag hole.

3. Rip handmade paper on all sides in irregular pattern ¼" smaller than tag, all the way around. Ink sides of torn paper brown.

4. Stamp fern images with both inkpad colors. Glue torn paper to tag and weight with book; let dry.

5. Ink sides of photo brown. Glue ribbon across bottom edge of photo. Let dry then trim off excess ribbon.

6. Cut cardstock to 3" x 3". Add double-sided tape around photo. Sprinkle on fawn or off-white glitter. Trim excess cardstock around edge of double-sided tape. Glue photo onto cardstock.

7. Ink sides of framed photo and glue onto center of tag. Weight with books to dry.

8. Glue seam allowance of bead trim to bottom edge of tag. Let dry 1 hour then trim excess.

9. Glue and sprinkle gold glitter in small spirals across bead seam allowance at lower edge of tag.

10. Embellish design in ribbon strip at top of tag with gold glitter. Add thin line of adhesive to bottom edge of ribbon and sprinkle with gold glitter.

11. Embellish design in ribbon strip at bottom of photo with gold glitter. Make glue dots ⅛" apart all around border of photo on cardstock and sprinkle on black or brown glitter. Add more glue dots in between border dots and sprinkle with fawn or off-white glitter.

Bright Idea

Why Micro-fine Glitter Works Best

Micro-fine glitter is ideal for enhancing vintage cards and tags because it shimmers rather than sparkles. It has a rich yet less glitzy effect. Micro-fine glitter also allows you to use a detailed piece of lace to make glitter lace paper that is very smooth to the touch.

CHAPTER 3

Flora, Fauna & Fish

We love nature and our animals. We love the desert and the forest, the mountains, our lakes, and the bountiful gardens. Oh, how they feed our spirit! We love our easy cats and silly dogs, our beautiful birds, and the grace of a deer. The flora and fauna of this great earth are so exciting. They enrich our lives in so many ways. Glitter personifies the dynamic colors of our forests, mountains, and rushing streams. Glitter adds life and love to every project. With glitter, we notice the details of an animal's coat, or the brilliant colors of fish. Glitter on flora and fauna is worth noticing and the largest boldly states, "I am." Glitter on flora and fauna projects communicates the delight we feel. Our animals make us smile and add so much joy to our days. From the goldfish in our homes and the wilds of our own backyards, to the wildflowers in a field, we can only hope to honor these beauties by presenting them in this chapter's exquisite projects.

Grapevine Fabric Card

Glitter

- Micro-fine opaque glitter: gold
- Ultra-fine transparent glitter: green, purple, tan

Materials

- ⅛" mounting dots, 3
- ¼" double-sided tape
- Adhesive paper
- Cardstock: ochre, white
- Clear-drying adhesive with ultra-fine metal tip attached
- Fabric: grapevine pattern, 8" x 10" swatch
- Fine-point scissors

Instructions

1. Remove backing from adhesive paper and press fabric piece onto paper. Cut out 4¼" x 5½" piece of fabric. Choose best composition of fabric, making sure to leave extra section of grapes and leaves to be placed in foreground.

2. Cut and fold ochre cardstock to 4¼" x 5½" side-fold card and adhere fabric panel onto front side with adhesive.

3. Apply double-sided tape around outside edge of front of card on top of fabric; remove plastic guard. Sprinkle on gold glitter to cover double-sided tape.

4. Draw some corkscrew tendrils with adhesive and sprinkle on gold glitter.

5. Choose cluster of grapes and leaves and one more set of leaves to put in foreground. Leaving ½" border around them, cut shapes out and adhere onto white cardstock with adhesive.

6. Outline individual grapes with adhesive then sprinkle on purple glitter; outline leaves then sprinkle on tan glitter. Trace some of veins in leaves with adhesive and sprinkle on green glitter. Let dry 1 hour.

7. Closely cut grape cluster and leaves. Place one set of leaves behind grapes and attach with adhesive.

8. Remove backing of three mounting dots and place on back, one on attached leaf and two on grapes. Apply small amount of adhesive onto opposite side of mounting dots after removing backing. Position grape cluster in center of card and attach to background. Let dry 1 hour.

Bright Idea

The Right Fabric

A variety of wonderful fabrics in every subject matter can easily be found in department and discount stores. For an even greater selection, be sure to look in your local quilt or fabric store. They usually carry very unique and beautiful fabrics that cannot be found anywhere else.

Fisherman Quilt Card

Glitter

- Micro-fine opaque glitter: silver
- Ultra-fine opaque glitter: black hologram, navy blue
- Ultra-fine transparent glitter: dark blue, dark green, warm yellow

Materials

- Adhesive application machine
- Boat, moon, and tree images (included in Clip Art section, pages 113-121)
- Cardstock: black, denim blue pearl finish, green, light gold pearl finish, medium brown, navy blue textured finish (2 sheets), pink
- Clear-drying adhesive with ultra-fine metal tip attached
- Embossing powder: clear
- Fine-point scissors
- Heat tool
- Inkpad: brown pigment, green pigment
- Pencil
- Rubber stamp: detailed leaf
- Scissors

Instructions

1. Fold one sheet of navy blue cardstock to 7" x 5" top-fold card. Cut pink cardstock to 6½" x 4½", cut denim blue pearl cardstock to 6" x 2". Adhere pink cardstock onto folded navy blue card with adhesive.

2. Cut second navy blue cardstock to 6" x 4". Adhere denim blue pearl stock to bottom of navy blue panel with adhesive, making a lake/skyline.

3. Cut out moon image traced on light gold cardstock. Adhere moon to lake line on left side of card with adhesive. Trace curve of moon in adhesive then sprinkle on warm yellow glitter.

4. Trace tree trunk on brown cardstock and cut out. Adhere to lake line on right side of card.

5. Cut leaf green cardstock to 2" x 3". Stamp leaf design on green cardstock with green ink then emboss with clear powder. Using clip art, cut out three green tree shapes. Apply adhesive then sprinkle on dark green glitter; let dry. Adhere to tree trunk with adhesive.

6. Cut four ¼" squares out of remaining green cardstock. Adhere to pink cardstock in corners with adhesive.

7. Apply adhesive on lake line then sprinkle with silver glitter. Make 1½" adhesive line on top of silver lake line positioned under tree to make shoreline. Sprinkle on dark green glitter.

8. Trace two silhouettes of boat on black cardstock and cut out. On silhouette, where men are facing to right, outline boat (not people in boat) with adhesive then sprinkle on silver glitter. When dry 10 minutes, fill in boat with adhesive then flood with black hologram glitter.

9. When dry, adhere glittered boat to lake line with adhesive, ¼" away from right inside edge of moon. Adhere mirror-image silhouette under glittered boat with adhesive.

10. On right and left sides of boat, apply adhesive to create wavy lines then sprinkle on dark blue glitter. Lines move from lake line to bottom right. Apply wavy lines of adhesive in same way then sprinkle on navy blue glitter. Let dry 10 minutes.

11. Apply wavy lines of adhesive to water then sprinkle on silver glitter. Leave blank space in middle of wavy water lines, where center of boat sits in water. Weight with heavy book.

Cat & Dog Gift Bags

Glitter

- Ultra-fine opaque glitter for cat: black, light gold
- Ultra-fine opaque glitter for dog: dark brown, dark gold, golden brown

Materials

- ⅛" double-sided tape
- Cameo charm or button
- Cat face image (included in Clip Art section, pages 113-121)
- Clear-drying adhesive with ultra-fine metal tip attached
- Gift bags: 4" x 5" brown paper bag, 2
- Inkpad, permanent: black
- Mat board
- Rubber stamp: large dog paw print

Instructions

Cat Bag

1. Cut mat board to 3" x 6" and insert it into bag. Using clip art as guide, copy cat face on center of bag.

2. Trace cat face with adhesive then sprinkle on black glitter. Fill in eyes with adhesive then flood with black glitter. Dry completely.

3. Add slightly angled slits in eyes with adhesive then sprinkle on gold glitter. Add double-sided tape to neck, remove plastic guard, then sprinkle on black glitter to cover. If using decorative button, snip off back loop. Adhere embellishment on center of cat collar with adhesive. Let dry 2 hours then remove mat board.

Dog Bag

1. Insert mat board into bag. Stamp dog paw print toward bottom of bag.

2. Fill in paw with adhesive, one section at a time, then sprinkle all three shades of glitter onto each section, darkest at bottom and lightest at top.

3. Write "Bow Wow" or dog's name in adhesive on top of bag then sprinkle on dark brown glitter. Make exclamation points, underscore, and curved lines around paw in adhesive then sprinkle on dark gold glitter. Let dry 2 hours then remove mat board.

Bright Idea

Applying Glitter to Glue in Time

It is important to get the glitter on the glue while it is wet, white, and shiny, between 15-60 seconds. Glitter will not stick well to glue that has started to dry. The amount of time it takes for adhesive to dry depends a lot on the thickness of the line, type of surface, humidity, temperature, and the amount of air circulation in the room.

Embroidered Bird Card

Glitter

- Micro-fine glitter: gold
- Ultra-fine opaque glitter: antique gold, aqua, black, brown, burgundy, dark blue, dark pink, light blue, light gold, orange, red, royal blue
- Ultra-fine transparent glitter: beige

Materials

- Adhesive paper
- Bird on branch image (included in Clip Art section, pages 113-121)
- Cardstock: nut brown, pink
- Clear-drying adhesive with ultra-fine metal tip attached
- Inkpads, permanent: brown, teal
- Pencil
- Rubber stamps: three different large leaves
- Scissors
- Transparency sheet

Instructions

1. Cut and fold pink cardstock to 7" x 5" top-fold card. Cut nut brown cardstock to 4½" x 6½".

2. Cut adhesive paper to 4¼" x 6¼" and peel off backing. Flood surface with beige glitter. Cut ¼" smaller than folded cardstock. Adhere glitter paper to front of pink cardstock with adhesive. Weight down with book.

3. Place transparency sheet on top of bird clip art. Using black glitter on adhesive, "embroider" outline of bird, wing, and tail and lightly circle eye. Place dot of adhesive in center of eye then sprinkle with black glitter.

4. Apply adhesive then sprinkle brown glitter on branch, and pink, red, and burgundy on berries. Fill in bird with adhesive then sprinkle on remaining glitter colors, using project pictured as guide. Let each color dry 10 minutes between color changes. When finished, let dry overnight. Closely cut excess transparency.

5. Glitter side up, lightly mark placement of bird on brown cardstock with pencil. Remove bird and stamp leaves on, around, and behind where bird will be. Stamp background leaves first with brown ink (they will not have glitter on them).

6. Outline leaf veins and leaves in adhesive embroidery stroke. Apply adhesive then sprinkle with ultra-fine gold glitter to highlight side of leaf and micro-fine gold glitter to highlight darker side of leaf. Let dry 30 minutes.

7. Apply adhesive to non-glittered side of bird and place in center of leaves.

Bright Idea

Achieving Embroidery Line

The goal is to make your strokes an even width about ¼" long. You don't want a line that is thick at the ends and thin in the middle. Practice on scrap paper. Touch adhesive metal tip to surface. Move to the right, the left, and then the right again in ¼" strokes. Skip about 1/16" from last stroke, and then apply adhesive in a line to the right to make a row of ¼" strokes with even widths. They should look like a line of adhesive dashes.

Rose Scrapbook Card

Glitter

- Ultra-fine transparent glitter: dark purplish pink, light green, pale pink

Materials

- ⅛" double-sided tape
- Cardstock: pink
- Clear-drying adhesive with ultra-fine metal tip attached
- Scissors
- Scrapbook paper: three-dimensional floral
- Spoon
- Vellum paper: leaf green

Instructions

1. Cut and fold pink cardstock to 7" x 5" top-fold card. Cut scrapbook paper to 6½" x 4¾". Apply adhesive along outside fold line of pink cardstock and inside fold line of scrapbook paper. Place scrapbook paper on top of cardstock, adhesive to adhesive.

2. With both still folded, push adhesive folds together. Let dry 10 minutes while in folded position. When dry, lift flaps then add thin adhesive lines to back of scrapbook paper, not to the cardstock. Adhere to cardstock and weight with book 5-10 minutes.

3. Apply adhesive then sprinkle dark purplish pink glitter onto centers of flowers. Outline highlights in flower petals with adhesive and sprinkle on pale pink glitter. Let surface dry 30 minutes.

Note: Apply adhesive then sprinkle on glitter as you go so adhesive stays very wet when glitter is applied.

4. Draw thin line of adhesive below floral paper. Spoon on dark purplish pink glitter. Let dry.

Bright Idea

Speeding Up Drying Time

Drying time can be reduced by shining a table lamp on the card. This will add enough heat without disturbing the wet glue. You do not want to use a heat tool to dry adhesives because it will boil the glue. Water-based adhesives should air dry only.

Bright Idea

Static and Glitter

Most glitter is made from polyester films. Polyester glitter will pick up static from time to time. To combat this, wipe working surfaces, spoon, trays, paper, and projects with a dryer sheet. If glitter gets static in it, it will stick together and fall off your spoon in little clumps. If this happens, pour your glitter into a coffee filter (they resist static too) and wash all surfaces, trays, spoons, and glitter jars. Let air dry then wipe with a dryer sheet. Put glitter back into tray/jar.

Cat in Victorian Window Card

Glitter

- Micro-fine opaque glitter: black
- Ultra-fine opaque glitter: gold

Materials

- ¼" double-sided tape
- 2" x 24" printed sheer rayon ribbon: green
- 4" x 6" translucent window stencil: 8 panes
- Adhesive application machine
- Cardstock: soft gold
- Cat image (included in Clip Art section, pages 113-121)
- Clear-drying adhesive with ultra-fine tip attached
- Decorative rayon/satin ribbon: gold
- Decorative vellum: embossed, tiny print, background pattern, gold hue
- Fine-point scissors
- Transparency sheet (letter size)

Instructions

1. Cut 3" x 3" piece of transparency. Place it over cat image and outline in adhesive then sprinkle with black glitter. Be sure to leave cat's bow clear. Set aside to dry 4-5 hours.

2. On back side, fill in cat's bow with gold glitter. Let dry 4-5 hours. Closely cut out cat. *Note:* Black glitter side will be the front.

3. Outline window frame with thin line of adhesive on one side of stencil. Sprinkle on gold glitter. Let dry 1 hour.

4. Place stencil on top of remaining transparency. On opposite side, adhere transparency onto window with adhesive. This is the "glass." Trim transparency to fit edge on window frame.

5. Cut green ribbon squarely in half. Add fine line of adhesive across top of window (on transparency side) and down both sides. Place extra-long pieces of green ribbon on adhesive, letting it overlap each end, covering up window. Let dry 30 minutes.

6. Cut excess ribbon at top. It will look like curtains are closed. Excess ribbon should hang (unglued) at bottom of window.

7. To make curtain "tiebacks," fold two ½" x 4" pieces of gold ribbon in half. Clip ends at 45-degree angle. Press curtains back with finger to fold curtains open. Position tiebacks and secure in place with adhesive. Let dry 30 minutes.

8. Trim drapes straight across bottom of window. Add very thin trim line of adhesive and gold glitter on every raw edge of drape, including window edges.

9. To make pillow for cat to sit on, put double-sided tape on one side of gold ribbon ½" x 4". Trim ends into shape of pillow. Apply adhesive on ends of ribbon then sprinkle on gold glitter. Let dry 15 minutes. Peel backing off double-sided tape. Adhere pillow to bottom edge of window with adhesive.

10. Add adhesive to back of cat (on gold-glittered side). Place cat on pillow and weight down. Let dry 1 hour.

11. Cut vellum to 5" x 8". Run vellum through adhesive application machine. On backing of vellum, trace rectangular shape of window stencil. Cut opening ⅛" smaller, all the way around, than rectangular shape.

12. Cut and fold gold cardstock to 5" x 8½" side-fold card. Peel backing off vellum and adhere to front of gold cardstock. Apply adhesive along edge of back of window (not curtain side). Place on top of vellum opening. Weight with book.

Vivacious Violet Medallion

Glitter

- Ultra-fine transparent glitter: 5-6 floral colors of your choice

Materials

- ½" mounting dots
- Adhesive application machine
- Cardstock: colors to complement glitter colors, 6–7; colors that match glitter colors, 5–6
- Clear-drying adhesive with ultra-fine metal tip attached
- Embossing inkpad: clear
- Embossing powder: white
- Fine-point scissors
- Heat tool
- Mat board: color to match overall tone of project
- Rubber stamp: floral medallion

Instructions

1. Stamp floral medallion image several times on various cardstock and emboss.

2. Cut out one whole image, leaving $\frac{1}{16}$" edge of paper around embossing. This gives weight to final project.

3. Begin cutting out other images in design. These images must be cut out very carefully against embossed edge.

4. Apply adhesive and glitter of your choice to areas that will show when image is layered. *Note:* Always apply darkest colors of glitter first. Try to match glitter color to paper color.

5. Place mounting dots on back of each cut image. Begin to layer by carefully lining up artwork with artwork underneath.

6. Run all square background cardstock through adhesive application machine. Mount background cardstock to each other and to mat board. Mount three-dimensional medallion to layered backgrounds.

7. A single-layer medallion may be used to make a greeting card or mounted on front of a journal or scrapbook.

Bright Idea
Mounting Medallion Pieces

For variety, images can be turned slightly or greatly to create entirely different designs. Sometimes, the very last little floret of a medallion is glued into place instead of using a mounting dot that might show. For a less dimensional effect, all pieces may be attached to each other using only adhesive.

Bright Idea
Cutting Medallion Pieces

The background medallion piece is the largest piece. It is the only one that gets an additional border. All other pieces are closely cut at the embossed edge. Accurate cutting is critical to the success of this project.

Fish Gift Tags

Glitter

- Ultra-fine transparent glitter: colors that match colors on fish (assortment of blue, green, orange, pink, purple, yellow)

Materials

- ⅛" hole punch
- Adhesive application machine
- Cardstock: tan
- Clear-drying adhesive with ultra-fine metal tip attached
- Fabric with 9-10 colorful whole fish
- Fine-point scissors
- Pencil

Bright Idea

Choosing Fish Glitter Colors

Use the same glitter colors that are on the fish or as close as possible. Since you are using transparent glitter, much of the original color of the fabric will show through the glitter. You cannot go wrong with this method. It is similar to paint by number because you apply adhesive to one colored section at a time and then sprinkle on the matching color of glitter.

Instructions

To Create Fish Tags

1. Run fabric through adhesive application machine. Separate fish by cutting out as many fish as you want for tags before removing backing, leaving margin of space all around fish.

2. Remove backing of one fish and position it on cardstock with at least 1" border above its nose. Press fabric down to adhere it to cardstock, smoothing out all wrinkles as you press.

3. Draw ½" circle with pencil directly above nose of fish. Using fine-point scissors, closely cut around fish, including ½" circle above fish's nose.

4. Punch hole directly in center of circle, creating tag hole. Repeat above steps with as many fish as you want for tags.

To Apply Glitter to Fish Tags

1. Use adhesive to create lines in fins. Put dots of adhesive on all their spots. Apply matching transparent glitter to lines and dots. Small sections of fish such as a gill or a mouth can be filled in solid with adhesive, then sprinkled with glitter.

2. Apply adhesive dots for eyes then sprinkle on glitter. Yellow glitter makes eyes stand out, though blue eyes work well too.

3. Fill around tag opening with adhesive and apply matching color of glitter. Let dry completely.

Three Tags on a Card

Glitter

- Ultra-fine transparent glitter: green, lavender, pink

Materials

- Cardstock: green, pink
- Clear-drying adhesive with ultra-fine metal tip attached
- Deckle-edge scissors
- Embossing powder: clear
- Heat tool
- Inkpads, permanent: black, brown, dark green, light green
- Rubber stamp: large floral, leaf
- Small strip of decorative handwriting paper
- String: tan
- Straight-edge scissors
- Tags: small, walnut-stained, 3

Instructions

1. Stamp 6½" x 4½" green cardstock with leaf stamp using dark green inkpad, leaving spaces for second set of leaves. Repeat on same cardstock using light green inkpad and emboss with clear powder.

2. Using deckle-edge scissors, cut front of card so there's ¼" border all around.

3. Brown edges of green cardstock by sliding across brown inkpad. Adhere onto front of 7" x 5" top-fold pink cardstock with adhesive.

4. Cut strip of decorative handwriting paper same length as green background cardstock and ¼" wide. Cut ends with deckle-edge scissors.

5. Darken all four edges by sliding across brown inkpad. Adhere strip across bottom of green cardstock ¼" from bottom with adhesive.

6. Place three tags side by side as though they are one piece of paper and stamp floral design on top using black ink. Apply clear embossing powder on wet ink and melt with heat tool.

7. Apply adhesive on small flower then sprinkle with lavender glitter, gluing carefully around black embossed lines so as not to cover them up.

8. Apply adhesive on middle flower then sprinkle with pink glitter, using same procedure. Cover last flower with adhesive and lavender glitter.

9. Apply adhesive then sprinkle green glitter on all leaves and stems.

10. After tags are dry, darken all sides of each tag by sliding across brown inkpad. Tie string through hole at top of each tag and tie in knot. Cut ends down to ¾".

11. Adhere three tags with adhesive to front of green cardstock, centering them on space left above handwritten paper, leaving equal space between tags and outside of tags.

CHAPTER 4
Seasons

Each year, the seasons take us through Mother Nature's yearly rituals. Spring—the breakthrough of delicate petals. Summer—full sun on the flowers. Autumn—amazing, colorful leaves. Winter—bright white dancing on the new snow. We expect changes and we enjoy the intimacy of those dynamics. Glitter helps capture the uniqueness of the moment as it highlights the unusual. It sparkles and reflects. It encourages us to stop and take notice of the detailing of our projects. A snowflake made with glitter flickers again and again. It doesn't have to melt and disappear. Our eyes catch the light and the color when we look out our windows at playful birds or when we walk down leaf-encrusted paths in the crisp fall air. The coat of a snowman dances in our eyes as we walk by. And the petals of a flower, shaded to create interest, encourage us to appreciate the beautiful hues inspired by nature. Glitter bridges a gap in our communication. It is the perfect medium to express what is special, brief, and unique. Join us in celebrating the seasons with these exciting projects.

Stained Glass Spring Card

Glitter

- Ultra-fine pearlescent glitter: dark purple, light green, light pink, lilac
- Ultra-fine transparent glitter: bright yellow, coral pink, light orange, lime green, pastel pink, periwinkle

Materials

- ¼" double-sided tape
- Adhesive paper
- Cardstock: lilac
- Clear-drying adhesive with ultra-fine metal tip attached
- Heat tool
- Inkpad, permanent: black
- Mat knife
- Metal ruler
- Rubber stamp: floral stained glass
- Scissors
- Self-healing cutting mat or mat board
- Spoon
- Transparency sheet

Instructions

To Create Glitter Stained Glass

1. Cut transparency sheet to 6" x 8". Stamp floral stained glass image onto transparency sheet using black permanent ink. Dry with heat tool. The side that image is on is the same side to do the glue and glitter work.

2. Apply adhesive on chamber where stamens lie and iris "whiskers" then sprinkle on bright yellow glitter.

3. To shade flower petals, fill one petal with adhesive, taking care not to cover stamp lines. Sprinkle on light pink glitter, toward center of flower. Flood surface of remaining adhesive with lilac pearlescent glitter. Repeat on all petals.

4. Sprinkle glitter on leaves and stems using two different shades of green, pearlescent light green and transparent lime green. *Note:* Do not add glitter to "glass" around the flower; this will look best left clear.

5. Start border by filling in two or three separated sections with adhesive. Spoon on pearlescent dark purple glitter. Repeat process using any other pearlescent or transparent colors. Let transparency dry overnight.

To Prepare Card Elements

1. Cut and fold cardstock to 5" x 7" side-fold card. Cut 4" x 6" window opening out of center of front of card with mat knife, metal ruler, and self-healing cutting mat. Apply double-sided tape around window opening, squaring corners. Remove protective cover from double-sided tape and sprinkle with pearlescent dark purple glitter.

2. Cut adhesive paper to 4½" x 6½". Remove backing and flood entire surface with coral pink glitter.

To Assemble Card

1. Cut around stained glass image so it is same size as pink glittered paper. Glue front side of pink glitter paper around border. Adhere glitter side of stained glass to glitter side of paper with adhesive. Weight down with book until dry.

2. Apply adhesive to edge of non-glittered side of transparency. Place transparency inside card and center it behind window. Weight with book until dry.

Spring Tag

Glitter

- Ultra-fine opaque glitter: green, pink, purple
- Ultra-fine transparent glitter: crystal white, light green, pink, purple

Materials

- ⅛" hole punch
- 6" x 6" piece of lace with leaf pattern
- Adhesive paper
- Cardstock: off-white
- Clear-drying adhesive with ultra-fine metal tip attached
- Fine-point scissors
- Inkpad, permanent: purple
- Pencil
- Ribbon: lavender satin
- Rubber stamp: small flower
- Tag image (included in Clip Art section, pages 113-121)

Instructions

To Make Glitter Lace

1. Cut adhesive paper to 5" x 8". Remove backing from adhesive paper. Position lace on adhesive paper and press firmly to sticky side of paper, ensuring all parts of lace are firmly in contact with adhesive paper.

2. With opaque purple, pink, and green glitter, sprinkle on each color, alternating like spokes of wheel until lace is covered completely. Tap off excess glitter between each color. Remove lace.

3. Carefully sprinkle light green glitter on leaves only. Tap off excess glitter as each small leaf section is completed. Flood entire surface with crystal white glitter. Tap off excess glitter.

4. Trace tag on back of glitter lace paper. Cut each tag shape out ⅛" smaller than actual tags.

5. Trace tag image on cardstock; cut out. Glue glitter lace tag to one side of tag. Punch hole through tag.

To Make Flowers

1. Stamp eight small flowers on cardstock using purple inkpad. Fill in petals with adhesive then sprinkle on transparent pink glitter, leaving purple stamp edge showing to define shape. Apply adhesive dots in center of each flower then sprinkle on transparent purple glitter. Let flowers dry 1 hour.

2. While flowers are drying, apply adhesive line along ⅛" border of tag then sprinkle on transparent purple glitter. Apply adhesive line around punched hole then sprinkle on transparent purple glitter. Let dry with flowers.

3. When flowers are dry, carefully cut them out with fine-point scissors, making sure inked purple edge still shows. Bend and shape some flower petals to give dimensional look.

4. Cut one flower in half and glue it on one side of tag, in two different places, at bottom right and at top left. Position each half against edge of purple glitter line so it appears to be disappearing off edge of tag. Glue two or three more flowers on same side of tag in random fashion.

5. For a finishing touch, run sides of tag along surface of purple inkpad and tie ribbon through hole.

Summer Tag

Glitter

- Ultra-fine opaque glitter: bright Kelly green
- Ultra-fine transparent neon glitter: blue, green, orange, pink, yellow

Materials

- ⅛" hole punch
- 6" x 6" piece of lace with large daisy pattern
- Adhesive paper
- Cardstock: off-white
- Clear-drying adhesive with ultra-fine metal tip attached
- Fine-point scissors
- Inkpads, permanent: black, brown
- Pencil
- Ribbon
- Rubber stamp: small morning glory with leaves
- Tag image (included in Clip Art section, pages 113-121)

Instructions

To Make Glitter Lace

1. Cut adhesive paper to 5" x 8". Remove backing from adhesive paper then position lace on paper. Press down well, ensuring all parts of lace are firmly in contact with adhesive paper. Flood entire surface with bright Kelly green glitter. Tap off glitter and remove lace.

2. Add glitter in spots then sprinkle with an alternating pattern of transparent blue, green, orange, pink, and yellow, where desired until remaining sticky surface is covered with glitter. Be sure to tap off excess glitter between each color.

3. Trace tag on back of glitter lace paper. Cut out tag shape ⅛" smaller than actual tags.

4. Trace tag image on cardstock; cut out. Glue glitter lace tag to tag; punch hole through tag.

5. Outline ⅛" border and punched hole with adhesive then sprinkle on orange glitter. Let dry.

To Make Morning Glories

1. Stamp three morning glories with leaves onto cardstock using black inkpad.

2. To achieve two-tone petals, fill in whole petal shape with adhesive then sprinkle pink glitter on outer edges. Then flood rest of glue with orange glitter. This shading technique calls for one glue application and two or more glitter applications.

3. Fill in leaves with adhesive and sprinkle on bright Kelly green glitter and a touch of yellow glitter.

4. Add tiny glue dots to center of flowers then sprinkle on yellow or orange glitter. Let flowers dry 1 hour. When dry, carefully cut out flowers. Make sure stamped black edges still show. Leave some leaves attached to flowers and take some of them off, cutting them out separately.

5. Cut flower in half and glue to lace at bottom of tag. Glue two more flowers with attached leaves on tag.

6. Outline ⅛" border around edge of tag with adhesive and sprinkle on orange glitter. Apply adhesive then sprinkle same color around hole.

7. After tag is completely dry, ink sides by running them over brown inkpad. Tie ribbon through hole.

Autumn Tag

Glitter

- Ultra-fine opaque glitter: dark green, dark orange, nut brown
- Ultra-fine transparent glitter: autumn brown, mustard yellow, pale yellow, tan

Materials

- ⅛" hole punch
- 6" x 6" piece of lace
- Adhesive paper
- Cardstock: off-white
- Clear-drying adhesive with ultra-fine metal tip attached
- Fine-point scissors
- Inkpads, permanent: black, brown
- Pencil
- Ribbon
- Rubber stamps: two different small leaves about 1" x 1½ "
- Tag image (included in Clip Art section, pages 113-121)

Instructions

To Make Glitter Lace

1. Cut adhesive paper to 5" x 8". Remove backing from adhesive paper and position lace on sticky side of paper. Press down and smooth lace firmly to adhesive paper. Make sure that all parts of lace are firmly in contact with adhesive paper.

2. Add glitter in spots, alternating with dark green, dark orange, and nut brown. Remove lace. Sprinkle entire surface with transparent pale yellow glitter.

3. Trace tag on back of glitter lace paper. Cut tag shape out ⅛" smaller than actual tag.

4. Trace tag image on cardstock; cut out. Adhere glitter lace tag to tag with adhesive. Punch hole through tag.

To Make Leaves

1. Stamp two leaves of each design twice on cardstock using black ink. Fill in one leaf with adhesive, trying not to put any glue over leaf lines. Spot glitter leaf in autumn brown and tan glitter, keeping some areas un-glittered. Fill in remaining areas of leaf with mustard yellow glitter.

2. Repeat same procedure on other three leaves. Set aside to dry 2 hours. When dry, carefully cut out with fine-point scissors.

3. Outline ⅛" border around edge of tag with adhesive and sprinkle on autumn brown glitter. Apply adhesive then sprinkle same color around punched hole. Let dry with leaves.

4. When dry, attach leaf from each design onto one side of tag with adhesive. Position them in different directions to create pleasing design.

5. After tag is completely dry, ink sides by running them over brown inkpad. Tie ribbon through hole.

Winter Tag

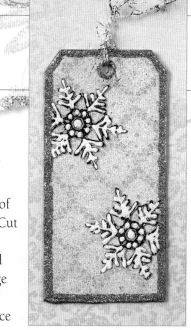

Glitter

- Ultra-fine opaque glitter: silver
- Ultra-fine transparent glitter: crystal white, dark purple, light blue

Materials

- ⅛" hole punch
- 6" x 6" piece of lace with geometric pattern
- Adhesive paper
- Cardstock: denim blue
- Clear-drying adhesive with ultra-fine metal tip attached
- Fine-point scissors
- Inkpads, permanent: black, brown
- Pencil
- Ribbon
- Rubber stamp: snowflake
- Spoon
- White-drying adhesive with ultra-fine metal tip attached
- Tag image (included in Clip Art section, pages 113-121)

Instructions

To Make Glitter Lace

1. Cut adhesive paper to 5" x 8". Remove backing from adhesive paper. Position lace on paper. Press down well, ensuring that all parts of lace are firmly in contact with adhesive paper. Sprinkle with transparent purple glitter. Remove lace and flood entire surface with light blue glitter.

2. Trace tag on back of glitter lace paper. Cut out tag shape ⅛" smaller than actual tag. Trace tag image on cardstock; cut out. Glue glitter lace tag to tag. Punch hole through tag.

To Make Snowflakes

1. Stamp snowflakes on denim blue cardstock with black inkpad.

2. Carefully apply white-drying adhesive then sprinkle crystal white glitter on each snowflake stem. Leave black stamped edges showing. Continue using white-drying adhesive on center, sprinkle with crystal white glitter, and add several small crystal white glitter dots in circle around center with same glue. Finish other snowflakes same way.

3. Using clear-drying adhesive, outline ⅛" border around edge of tag then spoon on silver glitter. Apply adhesive then sprinkle silver glitter around punched hole. Let snowflakes and tag dry 2 hours.

4. When dry, carefully cut out snowflakes, making sure stamped black edges still show. Attach snowflakes onto one tag with adhesive.

5. After tag is completely dry, ink sides by running them over brown inkpad and tie ribbon through hole.

Spring Gift Bag

Glitter

- Ultra-fine transparent glitter: blue, dark green, dark pink, pink, purple, yellow, yellow-green

Materials

- Clear-drying adhesive with ultra-fine metal tip attached
- Gift bag: floral pattern with embroidered butterfly in window
- Spoon

Bright Idea

Picking Your Gift Bag

Water-based adhesive will not stick to shiny, slick UV-coated surfaces. Do a test on the bottom of your bag to see if glitter will stick after the adhesive is dry. Some bag surfaces will accept the water-based adhesives but the adhesive may spread instead of keeping its raised form. Again, test the bottom of your bag before beginning.

Instructions

1. *Hint:* When enhancing colored bag, match transparent glitter colors to colors on bag as closely as possible. Work from darkest color to lightest.

2. Trace over butterfly with adhesive then spoon on blue glitter. Apply small adhesive dots evenly spaced around window then sprinkle on blue glitter.

3. Fill in dark pink parts of flowers with adhesive then sprinkle on dark pink glitter.

4. Fill in other pink flower parts with adhesive and pink glitter.

5. Fill in all blue flowers with adhesive then sprinkle on blue glitter.

6. Apply adhesive on purple flowers using small dots for little petals then spoon on purple glitter. Apply adhesive dots along vines then sprinkle with purple glitter as well.

7. Apply adhesive dots on vines then sprinkle on dark green glitter.

8. Fill in all or parts of light green leaves with adhesive then sprinkle on yellow-green glitter. Apply adhesive dots around inside of yellow flowers then sprinkle on yellow-green glitter.

9. Fill in following sections with adhesive then sprinkle on yellow glitter: petals of yellow flowers, alternating circles at bottom of bag, and decorative pattern at top of bag.

Floral Gift Bag

Glitter

- Ultra-fine opaque glitter: Kelly green
- Ultra-fine transparent glitter: hot pink, lime green, orange, yellow

Materials

- Brush marker: dark green
- Cardstock: off-white
- Clear-drying adhesive with ultra-fine metal tip attached
- Fine-point felt-tip pen: black
- Gift bag: medium or large, pink
- Heat tool
- Inkpad, permanent: black
- Light table (or window)
- Rubber stamp: broad leaf (or petals and leaves image included in Clip Art section, pages 113-121)
- Stem image (Clip Art section, pages 113-121)

Instructions

1. Stamp 11 leaves diagonally on bias of cardstock. *Note:* This will cause petals and leaves to curve naturally for three-dimensional effect later, after applying glitter.

2. Dry with heat tool. Reverse image on four leaves by placing blank side of stamped leaves upright on light table or window. Trace all lines with fine-point pen.

3. Make three leaves. Start with two leaf images that curve left. With dark green marker, darken half of leaf on left side. On one leaf that curves right, darken half leaf on right side.

4. With spout of adhesive bottle (metal tip detached), completely cover all three leaves with adhesive then sprinkle on lime green glitter. Set aside to dry. With ultra-fine metal tip attached, draw lines on veins and on border of dark green side of leaf. When dry, apply adhesive then sprinkle Kelly green glitter next to green veins and on border of light side of leaf.

5. Make eight flower petals with remaining leaf images (three that curve right and five that curve left). Fill surface of one petal with adhesive. Sprinkle on glitter: hot pink at end that attaches to stem, then orange with a little yellow on tips of petals. Repeat on seven remaining petals. *Hint:* You can use lime green on edges. Let dry about 2 hours.

6. Trace curve of flower stem onto gift bag. Position stem line so flower head will end up slightly off center, not too far left or right. Go over it with adhesive then sprinkle on Kelly green glitter.

7. In bold strokes, loosely simulate grass along bottom edge with adhesive then sprinkle on lime green glitter. Let dry 2 hours.

8. Apply adhesive to ends of three leaves. Let adhesive sit for five minutes and place ends of leaves at ends of leaf stems. To make leaves look natural, extend or follow stem line at center vein of each leaf. Let dry 30 minutes.

9. Assemble flower head on bag without adhesive. Place generous 1" dot of adhesive at top of stem. Let glue set for 5 minutes. For five background petals that curve left, apply adhesive to bottom of petal stem and insert at edge of adhesive dot. For three center petals that curve right, apply adhesive to petal end and insert into center of adhesive dot. Check position of all petals and make sure all petal tips are showing.

10. Add another dot of adhesive to center and sprinkle with yellow glitter. Do not tap this glitter off. Let bag dry overnight first then tap glitter off.

Organic Leaf Card

Glitter

- Ultra-fine opaque glitter: gold
- Ultra-fine transparent glitter: light brown, light peach, soft light gold

Materials

- Adhesive paper
- Cardstock: earthy brown
- Clear-drying adhesive with ultra-fine metal tip attached
- Decoupage glue
- Embossing inkpad: clear
- Embossing powder: copper
- Heat tool
- Maple leaf with stem: measuring 4" wide x 3" high and slants to right
- Paintbrush
- Rubber stamp: decorative corner
- Scissors

Instructions

1. Cut adhesive paper to 5" x 7" then peel backing off. Lay leaf on sticky side of paper, stem at bottom left with leaf at top right. *Hint:* Because leaf is not going to stick to adhesive paper very well, especially on delicate tips, extra adhesive is needed.

2. On stem end, curl back adhesive paper. Add adhesive to underside of stem, not to paper, and lay back down. Slightly roll back adhesive paper under one side of leaf, being careful not to damage it. Only ¼" of leaf edge needs to release from adhesive paper, just enough to get metal tip of adhesive under edge. Apply adhesive then pat leaf back into place.

3. Sprinkle center of adhesive paper with light peach glitter to create 1" curved stripe that mimics the natural arc of leaf, following stem and leaf vein. Tap off glitter, away from rest of exposed adhesive paper.

4. Along upper side of this peach arc, sprinkle on soft light gold glitter. Again, tap off glitter away from rest of exposed adhesive paper.

5. Fill in remaining paper with light brown glitter. Brush decoupage glue on surface of leaf. Let dry 30 minutes.

6. Cut and fold cardstock to 5" x 7" side-fold card. Emboss corners of cardstock with decorative corner rubber stamp and copper embossing powder.

7. Cut corners off glittered leaf paper to simulate corner design. Apply adhesive to back of leaf paper and adhere to center of cardstock between embossed corners. Weight down with heavy books. Wait 15 minutes.

8. Apply adhesive dots around perimeter of glittered leaf paper then sprinkle on opaque gold glitter. Add same glitter on embossed corners, highlighting a few areas.

9. Lightly apply adhesive to some leaf veins then sprinkle on gold glitter. If more glitter is desired, thinly brush on decoupage then sprinkle on transparent glitter of your choice.

Autumn Leaf Medallion Card

Glitter

- Ultra-fine transparent glitter: autumn brown, dark green, dark yellow, light beige

Materials

- ½" mounting dots
- ½"-wide ribbon: sheer sage green
- Adhesive application machine
- Cardstock: beige, black, ivory, sage green, 1 each; forest green, plum, tan, 2 each
- Clear-drying adhesive with ultra-fine metal tip attached
- Deckle-edge scissors
- Embossing inkpad: clear
- Embossing powder: gold
- Heat tool
- Mat board: nut brown
- Mat knife
- Rubber stamp: autumn medallion
- Scissors
- Spoon

Instructions

To Make Medallion

1. Stamp one medallion image on forest green, plum, and tan cardstock using embossing ink. Spoon gold embossing powder on each right after it is stamped, then melt with heat tool. Repeat process, stamping two images on ivory cardstock. *Hint:* The medallion on the plum cardstock is the background medallion piece. It is the layer that everything gets mounted to.

2. Cut largest medallion piece out. Leave ¹/₁₆" edge around embossed lines when you cut it out. This "frames" and finishes piece. Cut second image out of forest green cardstock. Cut out two large leaves opposite each another and keep the other two. Keep all four smaller leaves.

3. Cut same shape out of tan cardstock as you did forest green cardstock. When you mount this layer, you will be turning it 90 degrees, or ¼ a turn, so two large green leaves show from underneath.

4. Cut out fourth and fifth images from beige cardstock. Omit both of leaves on green and tan cardstock. One beige piece will include oak-like leaves.

5. On the other, cut off oak leaves and keep acorns. Each time you cut medallion layer, you will end up with smaller section of original image.

6. Apply adhesive to outer edges of plum cardstock then sprinkle on autumn brown glitter.

7. Apply adhesive to forest green cardstock then sprinkle on dark green glitter.

Bright Idea

Layering Medallion Pieces

When creating a medallion, stack all the pieces on top of each other to see how they look together. Check to see if each layer "peeks out" when placed under a smaller layer. Fill in, like a coloring book image, the shapes in the design that show when placed under the next piece. It is unnecessary to glitter each layer in its entirety because when layered most of the surface will be covered.

8. Repeat on tan cardstock then sprinkle on dark yellow glitter. Do not glitter one tan medallion piece.

9. Sprinkle dark yellow glitter in four corners of small piece to be placed in center of medallion. *Hint:* Do not cover embossed lines with adhesive or glitter.

10. Using mounting dots, assemble medallion. Place dots near edge, but not so they show. Peel backing off dots, mounting one layer on next.

To Make Background

1. Cut all cardstock for background as follows: black cut to 4½" x 5½", dark forest green cut to 4⅛" x 5⅛" and 5½" x 6½", ivory deckle edge cut to 2⅞" x 3⅞" and 4¼" x 5¼", plum cut to 5¼" x 6¼" and 3¼" x 4¼", sage green cut to 4" x 5", and tan cut to 3⅛" x 4⅛".

2. Run all background cardstock through adhesive application machine, or glue background cardstock together. If gluing, weight with book to dry. Without removing backing, stack background cardstock from largest to smallest on top.

3. Cut mat board to 6½" x 7½". Following our example, peel backing off ivory cardstock and mount it to tan cardstock. Continue to stack cardstock following the sequence of plum, black, sage green, dark forest green, ivory, plum, dark forest green, and then adhere whole thing to mat board.

4. Tie sheer sage green ribbon and mount on plum corner of background.

5. A single layer medallion may be mounted to make a greeting card or placed on front of a journal or scrapbook.

Snowman Gift Bag

Glitter

- Chunky glass glitter: black
- Chunky opaque hologram glitter: silver, slate
- Confetti glitter: white opal
- Ultra-fine opaque glitter: black
- Ultra-fine pearlescent glitter: pearl white

Materials

- Cardstock: rippled orange
- Clear-drying adhesive with ultra-fine metal tip attached
- Gift bag: black (not UV-coated)
- Palette knife applicator
- Pencil
- Scissors
- Small twigs with "V" shaped ends: 2
- Snowman and top hat images (included in Clip Art section, pages 113-121)
- Soft paintbrush
- Spoon
- Stencil paste: white
- White-drying adhesive with ultra-fine metal tip attached
- White tracing pencil

Instructions

1. Trace snowman and top hat clip art with white tracing pencil onto black bag. Leave space at bottom for greeting.

2. Brush thin layer of either adhesive or paste over shape of snowman. Let this base coat dry. Use white-drying adhesive to outline snowman. Sprinkle with pearl white glitter.

3. Fill in bottom section of snowman with stencil paste in small amounts. Use palette knife applicator to gently form soft peaks and texture, like icing on a birthday cake; be careful not to build it up too thick. While paste is very wet, sprinkle on pearl white glitter. Repeat on remaining snowman sections. Allow stencil paste to dry overnight.

4. With clear-drying adhesive, create two large dots for eyes and five smaller dots for mouth. Sprinkle on black chunky glass glitter. Using same technique and glitter, add three buttons to snowman's chest.

5. Trace top hat on snowman's head with white pencil. Fill in with clear-drying adhesive then sprinkle on slate hologram glitter.

6. Draw scarf around snowman's neck with adhesive then spoon on silver hologram glitter. After scarf adhesive is dry, add very thin line of black ultra-fine glitter on either side of scarf that flops over other end to create separation.

7. Using white-drying adhesive, draw large oval (snow pile) around bottom of snowman. Take metal tip off of adhesive bottle. Use larger spout on bottle to fill in shape. Sprinkle white opal confetti glitter on top of glue.

8. Apply dots of clear-drying adhesive in sky around snowman's head and body to resemble falling snow then sprinkle on white opal confetti glitter.

9. After everything is dry, glue small sticks onto sides of snowman for arms then add carrot-shaped nose.

10. Separate snowman's hat from brim by adding ¼"-wide hatband of ultra-fine black glitter. Add greeting by writing in white-drying adhesive then sprinkle on pearl white glitter.

Summer in the City Retro Card

Glitter

- Ultra-fine pearlescent glitter: coral, dark green, dark orange, dark purple, lavender, light blue, light orange, light pink, pale green, pearl white

Materials

- 5" x 7" polyester lace
- Adhesive paper
- Cardstock: bright yellow, red
- Clear-drying adhesive with ultra-fine metal tip attached
- Deckle-edge scissors
- Embossing inkpad: black
- Embossing powder: clear
- Heat tool
- Inkpad, permanent: brown
- Pencil
- Rubber stamp: retro of cocktails, drinks, beverages
- Scissors
- Spoon
- Stencil: oval

Instructions

1. Cut red cardstock to 4¼" x 5½". Emboss cocktail stamp design onto center of cardstock with black inkpad and clear embossing powder. Melt powder with heat tool.

2. Apply adhesive then sprinkle dark green glitter on olive and lime. Fill in liquid areas of drinks, one at a time, with different glitter colors of your choice. Let dry 2 hours.

3. Cut adhesive paper to 4¼" x 5½" and remove backing. Press and firmly smooth lace onto surface of adhesive paper. Flood surface with dark purple glitter. Remove lace then flood remaining white sticky areas with light pink, coral, and lavender glitter.

4. Cut and fold bright yellow cardstock to 5½" x 4¼" top-fold card. Cut 5½" x ½" strip off bottom of glitter lace paper. Glue it to bottom front of card. Cut two triangles off remaining glitter lace. Glue each corner to top of card.

5. Add fine line of adhesive along edge of glitter lace strip and spoon on light orange glitter. Repeat with triangles.

6. When dry, trace oval around cocktail glasses with sharpened pencil. Cut out with deckle-edge scissors. Ink edge all around by dipping it into brown inkpad. Glue to center of card. Weight down to dry 10 minutes.

7. Add adhesive dots, spaced ½" apart, around oval then sprinkle on dark orange glitter. Add light pink dots in between orange ones.

Bright Idea
Practicing Adhesive Lines

With just a hint of pressure, glide bottle tip horizontally across paper to get a little skipping of adhesive. Push tip into paper just like a pen. Add a bit more pressure to get a smooth, unbroken line of adhesive, the thinnest you can get. Then add more pressure with each line to see how many different line widths you can get.

Winter Medallion Card

Glitter

- Ultra-fine opaque glitter: silver
- Ultra-fine transparent glitter: crystal white, dark blue, light blue

Materials

- ¼" double-sided tape
- 5" x 6" netting
- Adhesive paper
- Cardstock: light gray
- Clear-drying adhesive with ultra-fine metal tip attached
- Embossing powder: clear
- Fine-point scissors
- Heat tool
- Inkpads, permanent: black; pigment: periwinkle blue
- Metal leaf: silver
- Mounting dots: 2
- Rubber stamps: medallion, small spiral
- Scissors
- Soft paintbrush
- Transparency sheet

Instructions

1. Cut transparency to 8½" x 5½". Stamp medallion onto transparency using black inkpad. Dry ink with heat tool, until it turns from shiny to matte.

2. Following our example as a guide, apply adhesive to stamped image then sprinkle on silver glitter. Try to stay within shape while gently moving adhesive to edge of lines. *Note:* Be sure to leave spaces un-glittered so lace paper can show through. This gives the medallion a light and airy feeling.

3. When you have finished applying silver glitter, sprinkle on dark blue and crystal white glitter. Let dry overnight.

4. Cut and fold cardstock to 5½" x 4¼" top-fold card. Using periwinkle blue inkpad, stamp small spirals along bottom and top edges of cardstock. Apply clear embossing powder and melt with heat tool.

5. To make glitter lace paper, cut adhesive paper to 4¼" x 5½" and peel off protective backing. Firmly smooth netting onto surface of adhesive paper. Flood with light blue glitter, remove lace, and finish covering sticky surface with crystal white glitter.

6. Cut lace paper to 5" x 3½" and attach to center of card with adhesive, overlapping spirals. Weight down and let dry 10 minutes.

7. Apply double-sided tape across card at top and bottom, where glitter lace meets spiral stamping. Remove protective coating and press silver leaf onto double-sided tape. Brush off excess with soft paintbrush.

8. Closely cut around dried medallion with fine-point scissors. Peel backing off both sides of mounting dots. Add drop of adhesive to one side of each dot then place both dots close to center, on glittered side of finished medallion. Add additional adhesive to mounting dots before adhering medallion to card.

9. On front side of medallion, put dot of adhesive in center and on four small hearts then sprinkle on silver glitter.

CHAPTER 5

Bugs, Beetles & Butterflies

The world of bugs, beetles, and butterflies is our world, too. How we enjoy a dragonfly pausing on a leaf or butterfly flitting by. In nature, real dragonflies have iridescent wings that sparkle and natural jewel-toned bodies that shimmer in holographic colors. A three-dimensional dragonfly in sheer film and glitter is absolutely breathtaking. You expect it to fly away. Dragonfly cards are sent as a well wish or as a thank you note. Any occasion is perfect. In this chapter you'll see how butterflies are set free from the background of a fabric card. It's so easy when the color is already there to follow. Two-toned shading makes them look real. Glittered bees on a gift bag are fresh and happy. Glitter takes any bug art from the ordinary to the extraordinary. This chapter features several regal ways to incorporate bugs, beetles, and butterflies into your gift-giving projects, bestowing upon them the nobility they deserve.

MOTH

ANTENNA

COSTAL MARGIN

APEX

FORE WING

OUTER MARGIN

THORAX
INNER ANGLE
ABDOMEN

HIND WING

INNER MARGIN

OUTER MARGIN

BUTTERFLY

COSTAL MARGIN

ANTENNA

FORE WING

FORELEG
EYE

APEX

VEINS

BASE

OUTER MARGIN

CLOSED CELL
ABDOMEN
SCENT POUCH

HIND WING

THORAX
INNER ANGLE

MARGIN

Butterfly Glitter Lace Card

Glitter

- Ultra-fine opaque glitter: black, gold, medium purple, pink
- Ultra-fine transparent glitter: light blue, pale pink, pale yellow

Materials

- 4¼" x 5½" adhesive paper
- 5" x 7" piece of lace
- Cardstock: cream, white
- Clear-drying adhesive with ultra-fine metal tip attached
- Fine-point scissors
- Inkpad: black
- Pinking shears
- Rubber stamp: butterfly (or butterfly in Clip Art section, pages 113-121)

Instructions

To Make Butterfly

1. Cut and fold cream cardstock to 5½" x 4¼" top-fold card. Stamp butterfly onto white cardstock, or cut out preprinted butterfly.

2. Outline butterfly with clear-drying adhesive and sprinkle black glitter onto butterfly outline, starting with thorax. Starting at top right wing, turn butterfly counter clockwise to outline next quadrant and so on, until all wing sections are outlined in black glitter. Let dry ½ hour.

To Make Glitter Lace

1. Peel off backing of adhesive paper. Lay lace over adhesive side of paper. Firmly smooth lace. Randomly sprinkle opaque purple and pink glitter over entire surface of lace attached to adhesive paper. Tap glitter off after each application.

2. Pull off lace to reveal lace pattern. Flood remaining surface with transparent glitter colors (pink, yellow, and blue) in random pattern, making sure whole card is covered with glitter.

3. Apply adhesive line to front top edge of cardstock. Attach glitter lace paper to front of card, leaving ¼" overhang on top and ¼" blank area at bottom.

4. Cut ¼" strip off bottom edge of glitter lace with pinking shears. Include front panel of cardstock when cutting off strip. Lift up glitter lace panel. With thin lines of adhesive added very close to edges, glue glitter lace flap to cardstock.

5. Glue ¼" glitter lace strip to bottom inside edge of card. Apply adhesive and sprinkle your choice of opaque glitter along decorative edge.

6. Apply adhesive dots then sprinkle on gold glitter to decorative cut edge of flap. Repeat on decorative cut edge of strip.

To Make 3-D Butterfly

1. Fill in spaces starting at top right wing with adhesive (top left wing if you are left-handed).

2. Starting at side of wing closest to thorax, apply thin strips of adhesive and sprinkle pink, yellow, and blue glitter so they slightly overlap each other. Repeat on all four quadrants. Apply adhesive dots to wing tips then sprinkle on gold glitter. Let dry about 2 hours.

3. To create 3-D effect, closely cut butterfly and clip half way between wings. Gently fold wings at thorax. Bend each wing around finger or pencil.

4. Apply adhesive to back of butterfly body and firmly place on center of card. Hold for 5-10 seconds.

Spring Moth Card

Glitter

- Ultra-fine transparent glitter: 4 different shades each of greens and browns, from light to dark

Materials

- ⅛" double-sided tape
- ¼" mounting dots: 4
- Brush markers: dark gray, medium green, ochre
- Cardstock: pale chartreuse
- Clear-drying adhesive with ultra-fine metal tip attached
- Heat tool
- Inkpads, permanent: black, ochre
- Metal leaf: gold
- Rubber stamps: floral border, and moth (or moth image included in Clip Art section, pages 113-121)
- Scrap paper
- Soft paintbrush
- Spoon
- Transparency sheet

Instructions

1. Stamp moth on transparency sheet with black inkpad. Dry lightly with heat tool until ink has turned from shiny to dull. *Optional:* Using moth clip art, transfer by tracing with fine black permanent ink pen or copying onto transparency with dry toner or laser copier. If you use a copier, make sure you have the right type of transparency for your machine.

2. On inked side of transparency, apply adhesive to thorax. Sprinkle one or two colors of glitter. Sprinkle bright green glitter onto desired areas of wings.

3. Sprinkle darker green glitter onto outside edge. Apply adhesive and sprinkle lighter green glitter to one wing quadrant at a time. Softly shade with several brown glitter colors, from light to dark.

4. Cut and fold cardstock to 7" x 5" top-fold card. Mask off card (cover with different sheet of paper) except for ½" at bottom.

5. Stamp on floral border using ochre inkpad. With ochre brush marker, add ¹⁄₁₆" thin line to create band along top edge of border. Add wider ⅛" medium green marker line. Edge green line with thin dark gray brush marker line. Repeat at top of card.

6. Add double-sided tape along thin gray line. Peel off protective liner. Pat gold metal leaf in place on double-sided tape; lightly brush off excess leaf with paintbrush.

7. Apply mounting dots to underside of moth and place in center of card.

Bright Idea

Advanced Glitter Shading Technique

To shade your Spring Moth Card designs, tilt the card with the wing higher than the thorax. Let glitter "waterfall" off the tip of the spoon. Work from the outer edge to the thorax. Slightly overlap the previous color. Let dry 4 hours. Closely cut moth when dry, separating wings to the thorax.

Flying Fabric Butterflies Card

Glitter

- Ultra-fine transparent glitter: blue, purple, yellow, and 3 other colors that closely match colors in butterflies

Materials

- ¼" double-sided tape
- Baker's parchment paper
- Brush marker: medium gray
- Cardstock: blue
- Clear-drying adhesive with ultra-fine metal tip attached
- Colorful butterfly fabric (with 6 different whole butterflies in assorted sizes)
- Fine-point felt-tip pen: black
- Fine-point scissors
- Fusible web or freezer paper
- Iron with non-stick coating set on medium-high heat
- Mat board
- Scissors

Bright Idea

Keeping Colors Fresh

Another approach to applying glitter is to start from the center of the fabric and work your way to the edge or from one end to the other end, changing colors as you go. Either way, tap glitter off, away from what was just glittered to keep colors fresh.

Instructions

1. Cut and fold cardstock to 7" x 5" top-fold card. Cut ¼" off bottom edge of front of cardstock.

2. On back of fabric, with 6-7 butterflies on front, iron on fusible web (follow manufacturer's directions) or waxy side of freezer paper to stabilize fabric. Tape this to slightly larger mat board.

3. Carefully cut out butterflies of different sizes, without antennae. Randomly place butterflies on front of cardstock. Spot iron to tack in place. Check position and make any adjustments necessary.

4. Cover with parchment paper and finish ironing butterflies to face of cardstock. If you used freezer paper, peel paper off and glue fabric into place. Weight with heavy books until dry.

5. Outline, fill in, or accent butterflies with wispy amounts of adhesive then sprinkle on your choice of transparent glitter colors. Starting with darker colors, apply glitter to thorax then wing sections.

6. Let dry 10 minutes and begin another color. Finish all colors; let dry 2 hours.

7. Apply double-sided tape to bottom edge of inside of card. Peel off protective liner and glitter with transparent purple glitter.

8. Apply adhesive dots between butterflies then sprinkle on blue glitter. Apply fine line of glue to bottom front edge of card and sprinkle on yellow glitter. Draw antennae with fine-point black pen.

9. To create drop shadow, use medium gray brush marker. Shade cardstock on right and lower edge of butterflies, as if sun was shining in from left side. If needed, go over shading to darken it.

Neon Bugettes Card

Glitter

- Ultra-fine pearlescent glitter: royal blue
- Ultra-fine transparent neon glitter: blue, green, orange, pink, yellow

Materials

- ½" mounting dots: 3
- Baker's parchment paper or non-stick ironing cloth
- Cardstock: medium green, neon blue, neon pink
- Clear-drying adhesive with ultra-fine metal tip attached
- Embossing powder: clear
- Fine-point scissors
- Fusible fiber: bright yellow
- Heat tool
- Inkpad: black
- Iron with non-stick coating set on medium-high heat
- Rubber stamp: stylized bug

Instructions

1. Cut and fold neon pink cardstock to 5½" x 4¼" top-fold cardstock. Cut neon blue cardstock to ½" x 5½" strip.

2. On front bottom edge of neon pink cardstock, cut off ¼" strip. Apply adhesive along edge and sprinkle on neon green glitter.

3. Stamp three bug images onto medium green cardstock using black inkpad. Coat black ink with clear embossing powder and tap off excess. Melt powder with heat tool until shiny.

4. Apply adhesive then sprinkle neon blue glitter onto main body of two bugs, and neon green in center. Apply adhesive then sprinkle neon orange glitter onto main body of third bug, and royal blue in center. Fill in remaining areas with adhesive and rest of glitter colors. Let dry.

5. Form 3" x 4" oval with bright yellow fusible fiber. Cover with parchment paper or ironing cloth. Press with hot iron to flatten for 5 seconds. Glue fiber to center of card. Let dry.

6. Closely cut out bugs with fine-point scissors. Apply mounting dot to center of each bug and arrange in row on front of card. Two matching bugs go on either side of single bug.

7. Attach neon blue strip along bottom edge of inside card with adhesive. Add adhesive dots along bottom then sprinkle on neon orange glitter.

8. Apply adhesive to bottom edge of card font. Sprinkle with your choice of colors.

Bright Idea

Practicing Adhesive Lines

Take a horizontal aproach to your scrap paper with a glue bottle. With just a hint of pressure, glide bottle tip across paper to get a little skipping of adhesive. Push tip into paper just like a pen. Add a bit more pressure to get a smooth, unbroken line of adhesive, the thinnest you can get. Then add more pressure with each line to see how many different line widths you can get.

Glittered Moth Gift Bag

Glitter

- Micro-fine transparent glitter: light blue
- Ultra-fine opaque glitter: dark blue or purple
- Ultra-fine transparent glitter: dark blue, orange, purple, yellow

Materials

- 4" x 5" fusible film: light-colored, 4 sheets
- 4" x 5" sheet of adhesive paper
- Baker's parchment paper or non-stick ironing cloth
- Clear-drying adhesive with ultra-fine metal tip attached
- Colored paper gift bag: small
- Fine-point scissors
- Inkpad, permanent: black
- Iron with non-stick coating set on medium-high heat
- Pencil
- Rubber stamp: large moth
- Stencil: oval
- Tissue paper: color that coordinates with gift bag

Instructions

To Create Moth

1. Ink rubber stamp with black permanent ink. Lay, rubber-side up, on table.

2. Carefully set four sheets of fusible film on surface of inked stamp. Without moving film, cover film with parchment paper or ironing cloth. Press and iron entire surface of stamp for 3-5 seconds with hot iron. Peel off fused film.

3. Apply adhesive to moth then sprinkle on opaque dark blue or purple glitter. Apply adhesive then sprinkle same glitter on thorax stripes, dots on upper wings, and dots and squiggles on lower wings. Rest of colors on moth are transparent glitter colors. Add glitter to any part of moth design as desired.

4. After moth is completely dry (3-4 hours), cut out image. Separate upper and lower wings by cutting in between wings. Bend up upper wings at thorax.

To Fill in Background

1. Remove backing from adhesive paper. While holding upper wings away from adhesive paper, attach lower wings and thorax of moth to center of adhesive paper. Flood adhesive paper with light blue glitter.

2. Using stencil, draw oval shape around moth and cut it out. Glue onto front of gift bag at top. Cover with parchment paper and weight down with book.

3. Apply small glue dots and transparent purple glitter around inside of oval. Work in small sections. Repeat with opaque dark blue or purple glitter on outer edge of oval.

To Finish Gift Bag

1. Write name of recipient in adhesive. Sprinkle on opaque dark blue or purple glitter. Like confetti, swirl line under name for dramatic underscore. Sprinkle on yellow glitter. Let dry.

2. Cut tissue paper into ⅜" strips. Separate and shake apart to make streamers. Put small amount at bottom. Insert gift and add remaining streamers, letting them flow out top of bag.

Transparency Card with Butterfly

Glitter

- Micro-fine opaque glitter: black, fuchsia
- Micro-fine transparent glitter: light pink

Materials

- ⅛" double-sided tape
- 5½" x 8½" transparency sheet
- 8½" x 11" scrapbook paper: heavy, textured petal pink
- 8½" x 11" sheet of adhesive paper
- Adhesive application machine
- Cardstock: lavender
- Clear-drying adhesive with ultra-fine metal tip attached
- Free-hand butterfly image (included in Clip Art section, pages 113-121)
- Masking tape
- Photo corners: black, 4
- Scissors
- Spoon

Instructions

1. Center transparency over free-hand clip art butterfly, then tack into place with masking tape. Outline and fill in head and body with glue on transparency and sprinkle on black glitter.

2. Trace shape of one wing using adhesive and scribble loose, smaller ovals over and over inside wing. Sprinkle on fuchsia glitter. Repeat on other wings. Allow glittered transparency to dry overnight.

3. Cut 8½" x 11" sheet of adhesive paper in half. Peel back off one piece of adhesive paper. Flood with fuchsia glitter. Use back of spoon to push extra amount of glitter into adhesive paper.

4. Peel back of remaining piece of adhesive paper. Flood surface with light pink glitter.

5. Run both pieces of glittered adhesive paper through adhesive application machine to apply adhesive coating to non-glittered side. Peel off backing from fuchsia glittered paper and apply to front of cardstock, cut and folded to 6½" x 4½" top-fold card, overlapping at top.

6. Adhere overhanging glitter paper to back of cardstock. Cut and fold pink scrapbook paper to 6" x 4" top-fold card. Peel backing, center, and adhere to fuchsia glitter paper.

7. Put dot in corners of pink glitter paper. Add black photo corner on top of each dot.

8. Trim transparency slightly smaller than size of pink glitter paper. Insert butterfly, glitter side down, into photo corners.

9. Apply double-sided tape to bottom front edge of card, trim, remove plastic guard, then sprinkle on black glitter. Fill in glittered tape with adhesive, being careful not to go to edges. Sprinkle on black glitter again. This makes strip at bottom very rich with glitter color. Let dry 2 hours.

Feather Butterfly Card

Glitter

- Micro-fine opaque glitter: aqua
- Ultra-fine hologram glitter: aqua
- Ultra-fine opaque glitter: black
- Ultra-fine transparent glitter: crystal white, light green, woody green

Materials

- 4" x 7½" sheet of fusible film: light green
- 8½" x 11" sheet of adhesive paper
- Cardstock: color of choice to match butterfly
- Clear-drying adhesive with ultra-fine metal tip attached
- Feather butterfly: large
- Hot glue gun and glue sticks
- Pencil eraser: small
- Scissors

Instructions

To Make Glitter Butterfly

1. Outline inner lines of wings and outside areas of wings with adhesive and sprinkle on black glitter. Let dry 2 hours.

2. Apply adhesive and fill in every other area in wings with micro-fine aqua glitter. Add three hologram aqua dots in corners of top wings. Let dry 30 minutes.

3. Fill in remaining areas of wings with woody green glitter. Let dry 30 minutes.

4. Apply adhesive and sprinkle on two rows of tiny crystal white glitter dots along bottom of all four wings. Apply adhesive and sprinkle on larger crystal white glitter dots across top of both upper wings. Let dry 2 hours.

To Make Card

1. Cut and fold cardstock to 7" x 5" top-fold card. Cut piece of adhesive paper to fit front of card with overlapping ¼" lip. Remove backing from adhesive paper and press down fusible film at slight angle across card. Cut off excess film. Sprinkle on remaining sticky surface with micro-fine aqua glitter.

2. Draw squiggly lines with adhesive across film. Smear lines in uneven pattern with small pencil eraser. Sprinkle on light green glitter. Adhere adhesive paper to cardstock, bending ¼" overlap across fold; glue to back.

3. After card is dry, attach butterfly to center of card using hot glue gun. Position at angle in opposite direction of film.

Buzzing Bee Card & Gift Bag

Glitter

- Ultra-fine opaque glitter: black, light gold, orange, tan
- Ultra-fine transparent glitter: crystal white, pale yellow

Materials

- ¼" double-sided tape
- 4¼" x 5½" sheet of adhesive paper
- 5" x 7" piece of lace
- Bee images (included in Clip Art section, pages 113-121): large, medium, two small
- Cardstock: rich yellow, white
- Clear-drying adhesive with ultra-fine metal tip attached
- Fine-point scissors
- Foam dots
- Gift bag: yellow non-coated, large
- Mounting dots
- Permanent marker: black
- Pliers: needle nose
- Ribbon: color to coordinate with bag
- Shredded tissue paper: light yellow or white

Bright Idea
Working with Several Bees

Complete the same step on all bees simultaneously. When you finish the first step on the last bee, the first bee will probably be ready for the second step. This will not only speed up the glittering process, it will also help you achieve a consistent look to all your bees.

Instructions

1. Apply adhesive on large bee's image lines. Sprinkle on black glitter, working in small sections. Let dry 30 minutes. Apply adhesive on bee's head. Sprinkle on orange glitter.

2. Apply adhesive to stripe at neck. Sprinkle on light gold glitter.

3. Use shading technique to make bee's body look curved. Apply adhesive on one stripe.

4. Sprinkle orange glitter onto both sides of stripe and tap off excess glitter, away from center, leaving it unglittered.

5. Sprinkle tan glitter onto remaining wet glue. Finish shading rest of body stripes using same method. Let dry 30 minutes.

6. Fill in spaces in top right wing with adhesive. Add small amount of pale yellow glitter to area closest to body. Flood remaining wet glue on wing with crystal white glitter.

7. Complete each wing section. Repeat same process on all bees.

8. When dry, closely cut and separate wings on body. Blacken edges with permanent marker. Bend up upper wing.

9. Glue body and lower wing sections to upper center of bag. Apply adhesive and add gold dots and swirls to bag.

10. Stuff shredded paper in bag. Place gift inside bag and add more streamers onto inside top, letting them billow out of gift bag.

11. Tie handles together with ribbon and tie into bow. Glue baby bees to ribbon ends. A matching Bumblebee Glitter Lace Card (see Glitter Lace technique, page 17) completes the gift bag with pizzazz!

Dragonfly Embellishment

Glitter

- Ultra-fine opaque glitter: medium lavender, medium pink
- Ultra-fine transparent glitter: lavender

Materials

- 4" x 5" fusible film: pale yellow, 4 sheets
- Baker's parchment paper or non-stick ironing cloth
- Clear-drying adhesive with ultra-fine metal tip attached
- Fine-point scissors
- Inkpad, permanent: black
- Iron with non-stick coating set on medium-high heat
- Pliers: round needle nose
- Rubber stamp: large dragonfly
- Wire: thin, bendable, black

Instructions

1. Ink rubber stamp with black permanent ink. Lay, rubber-side up, on table.

2. Carefully set four sheets of fusible film on surface of inked stamp. Without moving film, cover film with parchment paper or ironing cloth. Press and iron entire surface of stamp for 3-5 seconds with hot iron. Peel off fused film from stamp surface.

3. Apply adhesive on dragonfly head then sprinkle on opaque medium pink glitter. Apply adhesive on body then sprinkle opaque medium lavender. Apply adhesive on top and bottom of wings then sprinkle on transparent lavender glitter. Apply adhesive then sprinkle on opaque medium lavender glitter to create few small dots in some of non-glittered areas of each wing. Let dry 2 hours.

4. When dry, cut out dragonfly and cut between wings to separate. Bend up upper wings at thorax.

5. With pliers, bend wire into V-shape to make antennae. Glue antennae to back of head. Without moving, let dry 2 hours.

Gold Leaf Dragonfly Card

Glitter

- Micro-fine opaque glitter: black
- Ultra-fine transparent glitter: light gold, purple

Materials

- ¼" double-sided tape
- 3-D leafing adhesive with ultra-fine metal tip attached
- Cardstock: gold, light colored
- Clear-drying adhesive with ultra-fine metal tip attached
- Fine-point scissors
- Inkpad: light green
- Metal leaf: gold
- Pliers: round needle nose
- Round jewel casings: small, 4
- Rubber stamps: dragonfly, vine pattern
- Scissors
- Soft paintbrush
- Wire: thin, bendable

Instructions

1. Cut and fold gold cardstock to 5½" x 4¼" top-fold card. Stamp card surface with vine pattern.

2. Apply double-sided tape along top and bottom edge of card; clip off excess at sides and remove plastic guard. Sprinkle on light gold glitter.

3. Trace vine pattern with clear adhesive, then sprinkle on gold glitter.

4. Starting with thorax, trace outline of dragonfly with clear adhesive. Sprinkle on black glitter, then outline pattern of each wing. Let dry 1 hour.

5. Fill in wings and body with leafing adhesive. Let adhesive dry until it starts to turn clear. At that time, press metal leaf down onto adhesive and rub firmly. Using backing packed with leaf, your finger, or soft paintbrush, brush off excess leaf.

6. Cut out dragonfly and separate wings to thorax. Make antennae by bending wire with pliers. Glue antennae to back of dragonfly's head. Let dry 1 hour.

7. Bend upper wings at thorax. Glue lower wings and thorax to center of card on top of glittered vine pattern.

8. Glue two jewelry casings at outer tips of upper wings and two casings closer to body of lower wings. Put dot of adhesive on four spots you want "glitter jewels" to go. Let set 2 minutes before placing casings. Fill casings with glue and add purple glitter.

CHAPTER 6

Celebrations

Everyone loves a party! There is no better way to express a festive sentiment than with glitter. One can really get creative with a party theme. Use a little glitter or use a lot. The sky is the limit. When a bag, tag, or card is accented with glitter, the mood changes and the celebration begins. How wonderful to write someone's name in a sparkly spectrum of rainbow colors. Everyone loves to see their name in glitter. People see glitter and they say, "Wow!" Adding glitter to a wedding bag or an anniversary card expresses our immense joy for the occasion. We all rejoice in the birth of a new baby. By combining scrapbook paper and rubber stamps with glitter, we can easily create a unique "New Baby" card with the baby's name in glitter. It's a beautiful way to make a personalized gift that the new mom can keep and frame. Sparkle speaks from the heart. May the love, joy, and fun flow freely from these projects and inspire you to celebrate!

Gold Graduation Card

Glitter

- Ultra-fine opaque glitter: dark blue, light gold, or school colors

Materials

- Adhesive application machine
- Cardstock: gold
- Clear-drying adhesive with ultra-fine metal tip attached
- Corner metal embellishments, 4
- Embossing inkpad: clear
- Embossing powder: gold
- Graduation invitation
- Heat tool
- Mat board scraps
- Paper: white
- Rubber stamp: Congratulations
- Scissors
- Vellum: confetti, 2
- Wax-tipped tool

Instructions

1. Write name on white paper in adhesive, then sprinkle on blue glitter. Let dry 2 hours.

2. Run through adhesive application machine. Cut out name, leaving ¼" border at top and bottom and ½" border on either side. Adhere to gold cardstock with adhesive. Trim, leaving ⅛" border.

3. Cut out school emblem from graduation invitation. Adhere to gold cardstock. Trim, leaving ⅛" border. Cut two pieces of scrap mat board ¼" smaller than above pieces. Adhere to backs and weight down with book.

4. *Hint:* The finished front of the cards needs to be 2" wider all the way around than the bordered name and approximately 5"-6" high.

5. Add adhesive dots around edge of name and emblem. Sprinkle on gold glitter.

6. Cut vellum ½" smaller than front of card. Run through adhesive application machine. Adhere to front of gold cardstock. Add adhesive at edge of vellum. Sprinkle on gold glitter.

7. Apply adhesive to back of metal embellishments. Let set 5 minutes, until tacky. Place in corners with wax-tipped tool. Apply adhesive dots above each metal embellishment then sprinkle on gold glitter.

8. Position name on card to left side, tilting left side of name card down and right side up. Place school emblem, tilting it opposite way, at bottom right-hand corner of card, slightly overlapping name. Adhere into place.

9. Cut another piece of vellum paper ¼" smaller than inside of card. Run through adhesive application machine and place inside card. Stamp and emboss Congratulations in gold on white paper. Trim, leaving ½" border. Adhere to gold cardstock with adhesive. Trim, leaving a ¼" border.

10. Adhere smaller piece of mat board underneath and adhere entire assembly as inside greeting.

Recycled Gift Tags

Glitter

- Ultra-fine opaque glitter: colors of your choice including pink
- Ultra-fine transparent glitter: colors of your choice including crystal white, yellow

Materials

- ½" ribbon: pink, gold
- 5" x 7" polyester lace
- Adhesive paper
- Cardstock scraps
- Clear-drying adhesive with ultra-fine metal tip attached
- Decorative paper scraps
- Embossing ink
- Embossing powder: gold
- Heat tool
- Paper scraps: decorative
- Pencil
- Scissors
- Small butterfly image (included in Clip Art section, pages 113-121)
- Tags off new clothing or other items in different shapes and sizes

Instructions

Glitter Lace Tag (at bottom)

1. Make small piece of glitter lace paper in colors of your choice as described in Chapter 1. Be sure to use opaque colors on top of lace and transparent colors for remaining sticky surface.

2. Place tag on backside of lace paper and trace around it. Cut out tag shape and glue to front of tag with adhesive.

3. Add adhesive dots then sprinkle on glitter in contrasting color around edge of tag. Write name in same color in center of tag.

Scrapbook Paper Tag (at right)

1. Trace shape of tag onto scrap piece of decorative paper. Glue paper onto tag.

2. Outline some of designs on paper in adhesive then sprinkle on glitter in two or three different colors to accent tag. Attach ribbon as shown.

Butterfly Ribbon Tag (at left)

1. Cut adhesive paper ¼" larger than tag; remove backing. Flood with pink glitter. Trace shape of tag on back of paper then cut out. Adhere glitter paper to front of tag.

2. Cut piece of ribbon to fit down center of tag. Cut "V" in bottom of ribbon to make tail slightly longer than tag.

3. Trace small butterfly onto cardstock. Outline butterfly with adhesive then sprinkle on opaque pink glitter.

4. When dry, fill in butterfly with adhesive then flood with transparent crystal white glitter. Sprinkle transparent yellow glitter on body of butterfly on top of pink glitter. When dry, closely cut out butterfly then curve and bend up wings.

5. Glue butterfly towards top of tag on ribbon. Apply adhesive dots down strip of ribbon then sprinkle on transparent yellow glitter. Attach pink ribbon through hole.

Wedding Gift Bag

Glitter

- Micro-fine transparent glitter: crystal white
- Ultra-fine transparent glitter: crystal white, green, orange, periwinkle, pink

Materials

- ⅛" double-sided tape
- Adhesive application machine
- Adhesive paper
- Cardstock: periwinkle with textured finish
- Clear-drying adhesive with ultra-fine metal tip attached
- Gift bag: white euro
- Laser cuts: wedding cake image, wedding phrase
- Pencil
- Scissors
- Spoon
- White-drying adhesive with ultra-fine metal tip attached

Instructions

1. Cut adhesive paper to size of cake laser cut then peel off backing. Place back of laser cake panel to sticky side of adhesive paper. Carefully press all surfaces together. Flood with ultra-fine crystal white glitter. Tap off excess glitter.

2. With clear-drying adhesive, sprinkle same white glitter on top of cake, lattice on side of cake, cake base, and draping. Leave rest of icing on side of cake without glitter. Let dry 2 hours.

3. Apply clear-drying adhesive on every other mini flower and on garden lattice then sprinkle on periwinkle glitter. Let dry 30 minutes.

4. Apply clear-drying adhesive on every other mini flower on cake then sprinkle on orange glitter. Let dry 10 minutes.

5. Apply clear-drying adhesive on center of mini flowers, adhesive dots along top edge of draping, and on large flowers at top of cake then sprinkle on pink glitter. Let dry 10 minutes.

6. Apply clear-drying adhesive dots around base of each cake layer then sprinkle on green glitter. Apply clear-drying adhesive to fill in vines in background and to add tiny green leaves in flowers then sprinkle on green glitter.

7. Make draping on cake more dimensional by adding layer of white-drying adhesive sprinkled with ultra-fine crystal white glitter.

8. To soften color of garden lattice, apply clear-drying adhesive with micro-fine crystal white glitter on top. Add tape around cake edge, remove plastic guard, then sprinkle on more micro-fine crystal white glitter.

9. Lay laser-cut phrase on top of cardstock. Trace around, creating ⅛" bordered background.

10. For phrase, apply white-drying glue then sprinkle on ultra-fine crystal white glitter. On border of word, apply clear-drying adhesive then sprinkle on micro-fine crystal white glitter. Let dry 1 hour.

11. Apply clear-drying adhesive on flowers and leaves then sprinkle transparent orange on flowers and purple and green glitter on leaves.

12. Run both pieces through adhesive application machine, mount glittered phrase to center of periwinkle background, then adhere to gift bag.

13. Let laser cut images dry completely, about 30-40 minutes. Tuck lace, paper streamers, or tissue paper in bag and add gift.

Anniversary Card

Glitter

- Ultra-fine opaque glitter: gold, purple
- Ultra-fine transparent glitter: crystal white

Materials

- ⅛" hole punch
- ¾" decorative beige trim with mini pearls
- 9" x 12" detailed polyester lace
- Adhesive application machine
- Adhesive paper
- Brads: purple, 2
- Cardstock: beige
- Clear-drying adhesive with ultra-fine metal tip attached
- Embossing inkpad: clear
- Embossing powder: gold
- Happy Anniversary image (included in Clip Art section, pages 113-121)
- Heat tool
- Mat board scraps
- Scissors
- Transparency sheet (letter size)
- Vellum: festive

Instructions

1. Place half of transparency sheet on clip art of Happy Anniversary. Trace in adhesive then sprinkle on purple glitter. Let dry 2 hours or until adhesive does not show as white on other side.

2. To make glitter lace paper, cut adhesive paper in half then peel off backing. Firmly smooth lace onto sticky surface. Sprinkle on gold glitter, remove lace, then flood surface with white glitter.

3. Cut and fold beige cardstock to 8½" x 5½" top-fold card. Trim glitter lace paper to same size as front of cardstock. Run through adhesive application machine. Adhere to front of cardstock.

4. Apply adhesive line on front of cardstock, 1¼" higher than bottom edge. Apply center of trim to adhesive line. Let set 10 minutes.

5. *Hint:* To correctly position Happy Anniversary, center transparency on glitter lace panel between trim edge and top of card. Poke hole with pin at upper corners and just below edge of trim. Trim transparency to these marks.

6. Lifting upper edge of trim, apply adhesive to cardstock along first glue line. Snug bottom edge of transparency to meet glue. Line up upper corners with glitter lace. Let set 30 minutes.

7. Punch holes at upper corners and insert brads. Adhere undersides of brads in place with adhesive. Apply purple glitter dots across center of trim at bottom of card.

Embossed Heart Card

Glitter

- Micro-fine opaque glitter: purple
- Ultra-fine opaque glitter: gold

Materials

- ¼" double-sided tape
- Adhesive paper
- Cardstock: purple
- Clear-drying adhesive with ultra-fine metal tip attached
- Embossing inkpad: clear
- Embossing powder: gold
- Fine-point scissors
- Heat tool
- Rubber stamp: lace heart
- Scissors
- Three-dimensional embossing adhesive with ultra-fine metal tip attached

Instructions

1. Cut and fold purple cardstock to 5½" x 4¼" top-fold card. Stamp and emboss heart design in gold on remaining piece of purple cardstock using clear embossing inkpad. Heat with tool to melt powder.

2. Outline main patterns in heart with embossing adhesive, including all dots. Coat immediately with gold embossing powder. Allow three-dimensional embossing to dry completely, about 2 hours. Melt embossing powder over completely dry embossing glue.

3. Add gold glitter highlights to all dots and inside some of lines of design. Set aside to dry.

4. Cut adhesive paper to 5½" x 4¼". Pull backing off adhesive paper and coat sticky side with micro-fine purple glitter. Cut this piece of glitter paper to fit on front of cardstock with ⅛" border. Center and adhere paper to front of card.

5. Apply double-sided tape as a border all around outside of card, overlapping glitter paper. Remove backing on tape and sprinkle on gold glitter.

6. After glittered heart is completely dry, cut out using fine-point scissors and glue to center of card with adhesive.

Space Birthday Card

Glitter

- Ultra-fine opaque glitter: blue, fuchsia, gold, green, orange, red, silver

Materials

- Brush marker: dark gray
- Cardstock: blue
- Clear-drying adhesive with ultra-fine metal tip attached
- Embossing inkpad: clear
- Embossing powders: gold, silver
- Fine-point felt-tip pen: black
- Heat tool
- Rubber stamps: planet, space ship, starbursts, tiny stars
- Scissors
- Transfer paper

Instructions

1. Cut and fold cardstock to 6" x 3" top-fold card. Stamp and emboss planet in upper left-hand corner in silver and spaceship in bottom right-hand corner in gold. Write Happy Birthday on center. Stamp and emboss starburst and tiny stars around greeting with silver, overlapping ends.

2. Trace over first word in adhesive. To rainbow, apply glitter in stripes, lightly overlapping. Tap off between each color change.

3. Decorate spaceship in all glitter colors. Add silver and gold glitter to stars and starbursts.

4. Draw three extra moons freehand with adhesive then sprinkle on gold glitter. Let dry 2 hours.

5. Draw shadows under Happy Birthday, moons, and stars with brush marker. Fill in planet, stars, and shade spaceship with brush marker too.

Bright Idea

Shaking off Glitter

You'll want your glitter to fall off the card away from the rest of the glue. By holding the card from different sides, you can control the way the glitter falls off the card. This determines the angle of the stripes in the rainbow.

Retro Gift Bag & Tag

Glitter

- Ultra-fine pearlescent glitter: dark green, light green, orange, pink, purple, yellow

Materials

- Cardstock: purple
- Clear-drying adhesive with ultra-fine metal tip attached
- Curling ribbon
- Gift bag: green
- Inkpad, permanent: black
- Pencil
- Ribbon
- Rubber stamps: atomic design, boomerang/baton lines, star
- Scissors
- Spoon
- Tag: medium size

Instructions

To Make Gift Bag

1. Stamp large atomic design in center of bag. Stamp boomerang design all around atomic design, making stamp overlap edges of bag.

2. Carefully follow line of atomic design in adhesive. Apply purple glitter to wet adhesive.

3. Fill in every other boomerang in adhesive, leaving black outline showing. Spoon on purple glitter to wet boomerangs. Fill in remaining boomerangs with adhesive and apply light green glitter.

4. Apply adhesive on all sets of three baton lines and sprinkle on orange glitter. Glue all sets of two baton lines and sprinkle on yellow glitter. Glue single batons and apply dark green glitter. Finally, glue long, single lines then sprinkle on pink glitter.

5. Finish by making tiny adhesive dots all around and between designs. Glue and spoon on various glitter colors a few at a time to prevent them from drying out before glitter is applied.

To Make Tag

1. Trace tag on purple cardstock. Stamp retro star design in two different places on tag. Glue in first star and sprinkle on yellow glitter. Glue in second star and apply dark green glitter. Fill in circles with glue and orange glitter.

2. Apply thin line of adhesive around border of tag and around circle opening. Finish by sprinkling on purple glitter. Carefully cut out tag and tie onto bag with ribbon.

Personalized Baby Girl Card

Glitter

- Ultra-fine pearlescent: pearl white
- Ultra-fine transparent glitter: light gray, pink

Materials

- Brush marker: dark pink
- Cardstock, linen texture: pink, lilac
- Clear-drying adhesive with ultra-fine metal tip attached
- Decorative-edge scissors
- Double-sided tape: ⅛", ¼" widths
- Inkpad, permanent: dark pink
- Mounting dots: 4
- Paper: baby girl scrapbook paper with border and background print
- Rubber stamps: large lowercase letters
- Scissors
- Sheep image (included in Clip Art section, pages 113-121)
- Transfer paper or light table
- White-drying adhesive with ultra-fine metal tip attached

Instructions

1. Cut 1" x 6½" border from scrapbook paper. Cut 4½" x 6½" panel from center of scrapbook paper. Cut and fold pink cardstock to 7" x 5" top-fold card. Glue border to bottom of panel and panel to front of cardstock. Weight down with book 15 minutes.

2. With transfer paper, copy sheep clip art onto lilac cardstock. Trace over transfer shape with pink marker. Stamp name in center of sheep with pink inkpad. With clear-drying adhesive, fill in letters with pink glitter and light gray glitter for sheep's face and legs. Let dry 1 hour.

3. With white-drying adhesive and pearl white glitter, make fluffy oval shapes that almost touch each other around name on lilac sheep. With same adhesive and glitter, add pearl white dots to miniature sheep in border. Let dry 2 hours. Trim excess cardstock with decorative-edge scissors.

4. Apply strip of ¼" tape to background panel at edge of border. To create dimensional rope border, remove protective tape guard, then apply pink glitter to tape. Add adhesive on top and pink glitter again. Add another line of pink glitter along bottom edge of border with ⅛" tape.

5. Add glue dots to background pattern, then sprinkle on pink glitter. Let dry.

6. Place mounting dots on back of sheep and adhere to center of background panel on card.

Personalized Baby Boy Card

Glitter

- Ultra-fine transparent glitter: crystal white, denim blue, light blue, orange, yellow

Materials

- Cardstock, linen texture: light blue, light yellow
- Clear-drying adhesive with ultra-fine metal tip attached
- Decorative-edge scissors
- Double-sided tape: ⅛", ¼" widths
- Inkpad, permanent: light blue
- Mounting dots: 3-4
- Paper: baby boy scrapbook paper with border and background print
- Rubber stamps: large lowercase letters
- Scissors

Instructions

1. Cut 6½" x 1" border from scrapbook paper. Cut 6½" x 4½" panel from center of scrapbook paper. Cut and fold blue cardstock to 7" x 5" top-fold card.

2. Glue border to bottom of panel and panel to front of cardstock. Weight down with book 15 minutes.

3. Stamp name on yellow cardstock. Fill in with glue and denim blue glitter. Let dry 1 hour. Trim excess cardstock with decorative-edge scissors. Around cut border, apply thin line of adhesive and add yellow glitter.

4. On background panel, apply adhesive dots on pattern then sprinkle on yellow glitter. Let dry.

5. Apply strip of ¼" tape to background panel at edge of border. To create dimensional rope border, remove protective tape guard, apply light blue glitter to tape, then add adhesive on top. Add light blue glitter again. Add another line of denim blue glitter along bottom edge of border with ⅛" tape.

6. Fill in duck scarves with crystal white glitter and duck beaks with orange glitter.

7. Place mounting dots on back of name and adhere to center of background panel.

Bright Idea
Quick Drying Tips

Dry time can be reduced by setting your project a few inches below a 60-watt light bulb. You also can put the item on a window ledge in full sun for quicker drying time. To dry it even faster, set the project outside on a warm sunny day. Be sure to weight it down with a small rock if it is breezy so that your project doesn't blow away!

Button Card Frame

Glitter

- Ultra-fine opaque glitter: brown
- Ultra-fine transparent glitter: autumn brown

Materials

- 5" x 7" picture mat with 4½" x 3½" opening; burgundy
- Brush marker: burgundy
- Cardstock: light gray
- Clear-drying adhesive with ultra-fine metal tip attached
- Embossing powder: clear
- Flat buttons: assorted sizes in autumn colors, light to dark, pearlized
- Heat tool
- Inkpads, pigment: green, tan
- Pencil
- Photo album: brown leather-like cover, larger than mat frame
- Rubber stamp: leaf
- Scissors

Instructions

1. Cut cardstock to 7" x 5". Place mat frame, face down, on cardstock and trace mat opening.

2. Emboss leaves on cardstock using both ink colors. Write name or word in adhesive and flood with opaque brown glitter. Or, create art card with image to be glittered. With burgundy marker, color opening and side edges of mat board.

3. Add solid layer of adhesive on 2" around border of mat frame at a time. While adhesive is very wet, sprinkle on transparent brown glitter and push buttons into place. Add extra glitter if necessary. Repeat process around entire mat frame. Let dry 24 hours.

4. Glue art card onto mat frame behind opening then glue to album cover.

Bright Idea

Changeable Art Card

If you want to change the picture in the mat frame, glue the frame to the album cover first, leaving top of frame unglued. Cut art card small enough to fit in opening. The height of the art card should be approximately 5¾" so you can easily grab an edge to trade it out.

Cheers Card

Glitter

- Micro-fine transparent glitter: crystal white, pale gold
- Ultra-fine opaque glitter: gold, purple, silver

Materials

- Cardstock: black
- Champagne glass image (included in Clip Art section, pages 113-121)
- Clear-drying adhesive with ultra-fine metal tip attached
- Fine-point scissors
- Transparency sheet
- White opaque paint

Instructions

1. Place half sheet of transparency on clip art of champagne glass. With clear-drying adhesive, copy image and cover with opaque gold glitter. Let dry 2 hours or until glue does not show as white on other side.

2. When not quite dry, fill in glass opening with adhesive and sprinkle on micro-fine pale gold glitter (but not all the way to the top edge because the glass would be too full, theoretically). Let dry 2 hours. Closely cut glass and leave little extra transparency on either side of stem.

3. When front side is dry, turn image face down and fill in bowl, stem, and base with adhesive and sprinkle on micro-fine pale gold glitter. Let dry 2 hours. When dry, apply white opaque paint to space that is glass opening. While paint is wet, flood with crystal white glitter. Let dry 2 hours.

4. Cut and fold cardstock to 7" x 5" top-fold card. Arrange glass on left and write "Cheers" with clear-drying adhesive on right side; horizontally sprinkle glitter on word using opaque purple across bottom, gold in middle (from left to right), and opaque silver at top. Try to arc glitter to follow curve of word.

5. Add adhesive to back of glass along edges and to center of stem. Carefully place glass on card, not moving it once you have set it in place. Weight down with book.

6. For bubbles, add multi-colored opaque dots in champagne and floating up from glass. Add silver around rim of glass and base.

7. To make bow at center of glass stem, make two adhesive loops like wide "V." Then wiggle short line to make streamers. Sprinkle on purple glitter.

Party Birthday Girl Card

Glitter

- Ultra-fine opaque glitter: fuchsia, gold, light blue, red
- Ultra-fine opaque neon glitter: yellow
- Ultra-fine pearlescent glitter: lime, orange

Materials

- Cardstock: shiny purple
- Cardstock scraps, shiny: fuchsia, gold, red
- Clear-drying adhesive with ultra-fine metal tip attached
- Curling ribbon: lime green, orange, turquoise
- Double-sided tape: any and all widths
- Mounting dots: 3-4
- Pipe cleaners: lime green, orange, yellow
- Trim: shiny decorative

Instructions

1. Cut and fold shiny purple cardstock to 7" x 5" top-fold card. Cut scraps of cardstock into different sharp-angle pieces.

2. Write words like "wow," "birthday girl," "party," etc. with glue then sprinkle on any opaque glitter. Let dry 1 hour.

3. Glue on one long, angled piece of gold cardstock. Glue on pipe cleaners, curled ribbon, and pieces of decorative trim in random manner, overlapping some pieces.

4. Put mounting dots on backs of small pieces and adhere to card in different directions. Fill in blank areas with adhesive dots sprinkled with all glitter colors.

Bright Idea

Time to Glitter

You have between 15-20 seconds to get glitter on the adhesive while the adhesive is wet, white, and shiny. Glitter that has not been applied correctly may shed and even fall off your project after it dries. The amount of time it takes for adhesive to dry depends a lot on the thickness of the line, type of surface, humidity, temperature, and the amount of air circulation in the room. Keep these elements in mind when considering adhesive drying time.

We invite you to photocopy or trace the words, patterns, and illustrations on the following pages to create your own bags, tags, and cards. The sizes provided are exact measurements included in the projects throughout this book, but you can enlarge or decrease their sizes to fit your needs. For example, we used the cat on a gift bag, but you may prefer a larger pattern for a super-size greeting card, or a smaller cat for a gift tag. Enjoy creating your projects, and don't forget the glitter!

Born in Detroit, Michigan, Barbara Trombley is a multi-media artist, a visionary, and an entrepreneur. She has used her talents in a diverse spectrum of creative and business endeavors. These talents were evident from early childhood, when she astonished her family with her imaginative drawing and painting skills. Her first commissioned piece, at age 15, was a detailed charcoal drawing of a 94-year-old woman.

She formally attended The College of Creative Studies in Detroit, majoring in ceramics, watercolor, and fabric design. Exposure to various art media inspired Barbara to explore many facets of her imagination as revealed in her paintings, jewelry, ceramics, and rock art.

After college, Barbara worked for a graphic design studio as a lettering artist. She created signs, menus, logos, business cards, and ads for major corporations. After conducting a market survey for a sewing manufacturer, she designed a complete line of sporting goods bags.

For 20 years, Barbara created her own Christmas cards, each year in a different medium. In 1982, she used chunky metallic glitter and school glue from the dime store on the card. She was surprised by the amount of positive feedback she received, and a friend even commissioned her to make 50 glittered invitations for a New Year's party. This first order was the beginning of a future in the handmade greeting card business.

It took two years of research to develop Ultrafine Art Glitter and her Designer & Fabric Dries Clear Adhesives. These were used to create Northern Lights Cards, the first handmade all-glitter, all-occasion greeting card line in 1984. The business grew from Barbara making just a few cards a day to a company of seven women producing 1,500 to 2,000 cards a day and shipping worldwide.

After numerous requests, Barbara decided she would market her supplies to stampers and crafters. They wanted to learn "The Art of Glittering" so that they could use the same techniques to create unique and sparkling cards. After developing her own glitter colors, industrial-strength adhesives, and metal writing tips that are a part of The Art Glittering System, she became known as the "Glitter Queen."

Art Institute Glitter, Inc. now supplies artists and artisans, crafters and craftsmen with more than 375 brilliant glitter colors and industrial-strength adhesives. Her products have been featured on Martha Stewart's "The New Martha Show," "Home Shopping Network," and "QVC" and "Ideal World" in England. She frequently appears on the "Carol Duvall Show" on HGTV, demonstrating how to make glitter lace cards, Fabergé eggs and gorgeous layered medallions. Hundreds of retail stores throughout the world carry her full line of Art Glitter products.

In 2003, Barbara was given the Entrepreneur of the Year award from the State of Arizona. Since then, she has opened her own fine arts gallery next to Art Institute Glitter's showroom in Historic Cottonwood, Arizona. She is an exhibiting artist at the Sedona Arts Center and a member of the Color Marketing Group.

These days you can find her busy on her next work of art and, of course, developing new glitter colors. When asked about her success, she excitedly replies, "Do what you love! I love art and I love color and I love creating."

This book is a testimony to Barbara's dedication to art and glitter. She eagerly passes on her secrets to creating beautiful cards, bags, and tags with easy-to-follow directions. "It is my hope that these projects will prompt my readers to go beyond the techniques outlined here to create their own works of glitter art," says Barbara.

Barbara has inspired many people to take the ordinary to the extraordinary. Her passion and love for glitter has motivated countless others to reach beyond their normal capabilities and attain artistic heights they never dreamed possible. She has added sparkle to lives all over the world.

Credits

A Red Lips 4 Courage Book
Red Lips 4 Courage Communications, Inc.:
Eileen Cannon Paulin, Catherine Risling, Rebecca Ittner, Jayne Cosh
8502 E. Chapman Ave., 303
Orange, CA 92869

Book Editor:
Catherine Risling

Photo Stylist:
Annie Hampton
Rebecca Ittner

Book Designer:
Anna Macedo
Baton Rouge, LA

Photographer:
Zac Williams

Project Designers:
Debrey Taylor
Barbara Trombley

Contributor:
Emily Miller

Where to Find It

7 gypsies
www.7gypsies.com
Clock parts, scrapbook paper, tag book,
walnut-stained tags

Art Institute Glitter, Inc.
www.artglitter.com
Adhesive paper, Barbara's butterfly rubber stamp,
clear-drying adhesive, double-sided adhesive tape,
embossing ink and powder, fusible fiber and film,
ultra-fine, micro-fine, hologram, and pearlescent,
neon, vintage glass, confetti, glitter, leafing adhesive,
noodger, polyester lace, permanent inkpads, three-
dimensional embossing adhesive, transparency sheets,
ultra-fine metal tip, wax tip tool, white-drying adhesive

Comotion Rubber Stamps
Tucson, AZ
Floral rubber stamp

Creative Co-op Inc.
www.creativecoop.com
Creative elements feather butterfly

Embossing Arts Co.
www.embossingarts.com
Leaves rubber stamps

Fiskars
www.fiskars.com
Decorative-edge scissors

Frances Meyer Inc.
www.francesmeyer.com
Scrapbook papers

Fred B. Mullett
www.fredbmullett.com
Leaves rubber stamps

Hero Arts
www.heroarts.com
Butterflies and leaves rubber stamps

Holly Berry House
www.hollyberryhouse.com
Three-flowers, bug, medallions,
and moth rubber stamps

Hot Potatoes
www.hotpotatoes.com
Atomic, boomerang, cocktails, retro bug,
retro dragonfly, and retro star rubber stamps

Impress Rubber Stamps
www.impressrubberstamps.com
Diamond pattern rubber stamp #F4759

Julie A. Olson of Hugs & Stitches Quilts
www.hugsandstitchesquilts.com
Me & My Shadow appliqué wall quilt design

Just For Fun Rubber Stamps
www.jffstamps.com
Postal rubber stamps

Laser Works, Inc.
www.scrapbookkeeping.com
Cardeaux Trimmings laser-cut stencils

Milwaukee
MHT 1400 heat tool

Paper Adventures
www.paperadventures.com
Scrapbook papers

Paper Parachute
www.paperparachute.com
Floral pattern and leaf rubber stamps

Paula Best

www.paulabest.com

Small spiral rubber stamp

Stamp Francisco

www.stampfrancisco.com

Fern, frame, plant, snowflake,
and vine pattern rubber stamps

Stampendous

www.stampendous.com

Stick-on copper letters,
P001 Christmas Tree rubber stamp

Stamper's Anonymous

www.stampersanonymous.com

Celtic, clocks, floral border with words,
frame with writing, patterns, postal, small tags,
and word rubber stamps

Stamping Bug

www.stampingbug.com

"Congratulations," decorative corner,
and dragonfly rubber stamps

Sugar Loaf Products

www.sugarloafproducts.com

"Whispers" cat face rubber stamp

The Cottage Stamper, Inc.

www.thecottagestamper.com

Lace heart and stained glass irises rubber stamps

Wildlife Enterprise Ltd.

Elk rubber stamp

Xyron

www.xyron.com

Xyron 850 adhesive application
and laminating machine

METRIC EQUIVALENCY CHARTS

inches to millimeters and centimeters

mm-millimeters   cm-centimeters

inches	mm	cm	inches	cm	inches	cm
1/8	3	0.3	9	22.9	30	76.2
1/4	6	0.6	10	25.4	31	78.7
1/2	13	1.3	12	30.5	33	83.8
5/8	16	1.6	13	33.0	34	86.4
3/4	19	1.9	14	35.6	35	88.9
7/8	22	2.2	15	38.1	36	91.4
1	25	2.5	16	40.6	37	94.0
1 1/4	32	3.2	17	43.2	38	96.5
1 1/2	38	3.8	18	45.7	39	99.1
1 3/4	44	4.4	19	48.3	40	101.6
2	51	5.1	20	50.8	41	104.1
2 1/2	64	6.4	21	53.3	42	106.7
3	76	7.6	22	55.9	43	109.2
3 1/2	89	8.9	23	58.4	44	111.8
4	102	10.2	24	61.0	45	114.3
4 1/2	114	11.4	25	63.5	46	116.8
5	127	12.7	26	66.0	47	119.4
6	152	15.2	27	68.6	48	121.9
7	178	17.8	28	71.1	49	124.5
8	203	20.3	29	73.7	50	127.0

yards to meters

yards	meters	yards	meters	yards	meters	yards	meters	yards	meters
1/8	0.11	2 1/8	1.94	4 1/8	3.77	6 1/8	5.60	8 1/8	7.43
1/4	0.23	2 1/4	2.06	4 1/4	3.89	6 1/4	5.72	8 1/4	7.54
3/8	0.34	2 3/8	2.17	4 3/8	4.00	6 3/8	5.83	8 3/8	7.66
1/2	0.46	2 1/2	2.29	4 1/2	4.11	6 1/2	5.94	8 1/2	7.77
5/8	0.57	2 5/8	2.40	4 5/8	4.23	6 5/8	6.06	8 5/8	7.89
3/4	0.69	2 3/4	2.51	4 3/4	4.34	6 3/4	6.17	8 3/4	8.00
7/8	0.80	2 7/8	2.63	4 7/8	4.46	6 7/8	6.29	8 7/8	8.12
1	0.91	3	2.74	5	4.57	7	6.40	9	8.23
1 1/8	1.03	3 1/8	2.86	5 1/8	4.69	7 1/8	6.52	9 1/8	8.34
1 1/4	1.14	3 1/4	2.97	5 1/4	4.80	7 1/4	6.63	9 1/4	8.46
1 3/8	1.26	3 3/8	3.09	5 3/8	4.91	7 3/8	6.74	9 3/8	8.57
1 1/2	1.37	3 1/2	3.20	5 1/2	5.03	7 1/2	6.86	9 1/2	8.69
1 5/8	1.49	3 5/8	3.31	5 5/8	5.14	7 5/8	6.97	9 5/8	8.80
1 3/4	1.60	3 3/4	3.43	5 3/4	5.26	7 3/4	7.09	9 3/4	8.92
1 7/8	1.71	3 7/8	3.54	5 7/8	5.37	7 7/8	7.20	9 7/8	9.03
2	1.83	4	3.66	6	5.49	8	7.32	10	9.14

Index